Everett Lee Hunt

Dedicated to
the family of Everett Lee Hunt
and all others who share
his humanistic spirit

Rhetoric as a Human Adventure:

A Short Biography of Everett Lee Hunt

Theodore Otto Windt, Jr.

Published by the
Speech Communication Association
Annandale, Virginia
1990

Library of Congress Catalog Card Number: 90-062919
ISBN: 0-944811-04-3

First published in November 1990

Speech Communication Association, 5105 Backlick Road, Building E, Annandale, VA 22003

Printed in the United States of America.

Contents

Foreword

Should the discipline of speech communication define itself primarily in terms of scholarship or education? Is communication best studied from a scientific or a humanistic perspective? Should the object of study be the form or the content of messages? Members of the Speech Communication Association feel strongly about these and similar questions, and their responses to them continue to fill journal pages and convention programs.

Previous Histories of the Discipline and Association

The Speech Communication Association (SCA) has addressed such questions in several published volumes devoted to the history of the discipline and of the Association. Some of these histories have focused upon contemporary and historical public addresses. Others have emphasized the origins and evolution of the discipline. Some have celebrated major landmarks in the history of SCA.

These histories first appeared in the early 1940s and 1950s. In 1943, the two volume *A History of American Public Address*, edited by William Norwood Brigance, was published under the auspices of SCA. In the mid-1950s, two additional historical volumes were published under the Association's auspices. Under the editorship of Karl R. Wallace, *History of Speech Education in America* was published in 1954, and under the editorship of Marie Kathryn Hochmuth [Nicholas], the third volume of *A History of and Criticism of American Public Address* was published in 1955.

In 1964, SCA's 50th anniversary constituted a time for reflecting upon the history of the Association. The *Quarterly Journal of Speech* devoted pages to this landmark in the history of the Association. For example, in his essay, "The Founding of the Speech Association of America: Happy Birthday," Giles W. Gray recaptured the historical moments which gave birth to the Speech Communication Association, and in "A History of the Speech Association of America, 1914-1964," Robert C. Jeffrey reviewed specific patterns of growth and development in the Association. The Association also published *Speech Communication of American Golden Anniversary 1964* which included contemporary articles and several reprints from the *Quarterly Journal of Speech* which captured the history of the Association.

The year 1989 marked the 75th anniversary of the Association and provided another opportunity for reflection. SCA again sponsored the publication of two volumes. Edited by Gerald M. Phillips and Julia A. Wood, the first volume is aptly entitled *Speech Communication: Essays to Commemorate the 75th Anniversary of The Speech Communication Association* and provides a series of state-of-the-art-reviews of major content areas defining the discipline of speech communication. The second volume focused upon the history of SCA, was edited by William Work and Robert C. Jeffrey, and was appropriately entitled *The Past Is Prologue: A 75th Anniversary Publication of the Speech Communication Association*.

Finally, SCA's 75th Anniversary was noted by a special retrospective issue of *Time* magazine, titled *Communication 1940-1989*. The magazine includes news accounts and photographs of significant events in the history of communication. The articles and photos were selected from the *Time* magazine archives and related to the history of the discipline by J. Jeffery Auer, Robert C. Jeffrey, Gerald R. Miller, Patti P. Gillespie, and Carolyn Calloway-Thomas.

A Short Biography of Everett Lee Hunt

While these earlier historical efforts provide insightful views of the development of the discipline and the Association, SCA would negligent if it failed to record important contributions made to the discipline and to the Association by specific individuals.

Thus, SCA's 75th anniversary provides an opportunity to publish Theodore Otto Windt, Jr.'s *Rhetoric as a Human Adventure: A Short Biography of Everett Lee Hunt*. *Rhetoric as a Human Adventure* traces the intellectual and professional growth of a man who began as a teacher of oratory and a coach of debate at a small sectarian college in North Dakota, matured at the Cornell School of Rhetoric and ended his career as Dean of Swarthmore. Along the way he actively participated in the debates that helped to shape our discipline and our Association.

Theodore Otto Windt, Jr. opens this biography with a sketch of Hunt as a friend. He turns quickly, however, to a description of Hunt's development as an educator and as a scholar. The second chapter provides an account of the youthful ambition and intellectual curiosity that drove a young Professor Hunt from his home in the windy plains of the West to the stimulating intellectual atmosphere at the Cornell School of Rhetoric. While in Ithaca, we are given a sense that Hunt began to focus his ideas and temper his professional drive through repeated public debates over important changes in the discipline. Finally, we see Hunt find a second home at Swarthmore and observe his participation in its unique educational atmosphere.

While *Rhetoric as a Human Adventure* is primarily Windt's accounting of Hunt's professional development, the author also provides glimpses of a remarkable humanitarian. The reader can sense the professional and personal choices Hunt must have struggled with as he moved from Huron College to Cornell and then to Swarthmore. Mostly, Hunt's consistent commitment to the principles of humanistic rhetoric provide the canvas upon which Windt is able to paint Hunt as an educator and scholar.

Windt describes Hunt as an intellectual who felt strongly about education and humanistic principles of communication, and Hunt apparently lived his life accordingly. While Hunt may not have influenced the discipline and the Association as much as he would have liked, *Rhetoric as a Human Adventure* leaves little doubt that Hunt left his mark on what he cared most about—his students.

Windt writes of a man who was part teacher and part preacher and who was totally a humanistic scholar. Hunt is presented as a man who lived what he taught and what he wrote—that dichotomizing scholarship and education is unnecessary.

James L. Gaudino
Executive Director
Speech Communication Association
August 1990

Preface

The year 1990 marked the centennial of Everett Lee Hunt's birth. It was with that landmark in mind that this short biography of his career as a teacher and rhetorician was written. *Rhetoric as a Human Adventure* is not a full-dressed biography of the life of Everett Hunt. Such a task is beyond my scope and ken. It would take someone who knew him well during his days as Dean of Swarthmore to do that.

Instead, this short book concentrates on Hunt's career as a rhetorician and teacher. He began as a teacher of oratory and debate at a small sectarian college, moved to Ithaca where he helped shape the Cornell School of Rhetoric, and then went to Swarthmore where he taught public speaking and coached debate before settling into his career as Professor of English and later Dean of the College. In tracing his teaching career I have taken some side excursions to provide brief summaries of the background of the colleges and departments in which he taught and to sketch some of the colleagues with whom he worked. This book also follows the development of his thinking about the place of humane rhetoric in the modern world which was one principal theme in all his writing. Everett began writing essays about public speaking and rhetoric at the time when teachers of these subjects had broken away from English Departments and were forming their own professional organizations and departments. He played a major role in defining the central issues in those early days from 1915 to 1925. Though his ideas did not prevail within the profession, he had a lasting influence on some he was associated with and still others who came after him. Much of his writing was polemical. He produced only three sustained pieces of what could be called modern scholarship.

By temperament and inclination, he was a man of letters, and his ideas and style exhibit this. He wrote in the tradition of nineteenth century essayists rather than in the tradition of twentieth century scholarship. Therefore, I have quoted extensively from his work to let him speak for himself in his own unique way, a way that combines a clarity of thought with a felicitous literary style.

But such a book as this, limited as it is in focus, would be incomplete without touching upon the personal side of Everett Hunt that affected so many people individually. In fact, his personal knack of guiding people by gentle suggestion and genuine concern was his singular mark on others. But I really mean something more than "personality" or "temperament" when writing about Everett. It was his character that left enduring marks. He was, in many ways, an intellectual minister whose approach was humanistic rather than strictly spiritual or narrowly intellectual. Since he had the remarkable ability to adapt to the ideas and concerns of others without losing his own in the process, each person who came in contact with him often saw his or her relationship with him differently.

I fear that some Swarthmore alumni may be disappointed that more personal details and examples of his work with students are not included in this little book. However, I hope that they will gain a better understanding of why he had the academic reputation he had and that the few stories retold here will spark memories of their own stories and anecdotes about Everett. In addition, I have sought to capture one small part of his personal side in the opening chapter, "Sketch of a Friendship." Others certainly could write similar chapters that would cast different lights on his warm and tender person. I open with this unusual chapter to shed only one ray upon him as a way of inviting the reader to come to know Everett Hunt as I knew him. The remainder of the book charts his teaching and writing career.

The title, *Rhetoric as a Human Adventure*, came from Jack Powell who suggested it long ago as the appropriate description for Everett's work. I agree and believe it describes his life as well.

Sources

The primary sources are Everett's published and unpublished writings, clippings from newspapers and alumni magazines that he carefully kept, several tape recordings he made, his letters, my own research, and our conversations over the years. Everett wrote out several autobiographical statements and during his last years put together a bibliography of some of his writing. He also kept many of his manuscripts in order, with the notable omissions mentioned in a moment.

For his early days and his sojourn at Huron College, I am indebted to a number of sources. Everett kept a little notebook of his college days, entitled "In the Days of My Youth," and it survived. He also keep his yearbooks and a variety of clippings from the school paper and local papers. Donald W. Rasmussen's master's thesis, *A History of Speech Education* at Huron College 1883-1943, written at the University of South Dakota (1949), is an excellent survey of the subject and was most helpful.

His years at Cornell, the most important for members of the rhetoric and communication profession, were also the most difficult. No letters survive from this period nor did he keep any of his manuscripts. Alan Hunt, his son, speculated that they were lost or destroyed when his father moved in 1959 to 221 North Princeton Avenue in Swarthmore. The only letters from Cornell friends that survive are from the late nineteen-fifties onward, and I found most of them in books written by these friends where he invariably put correspondence from authors.

There are two important sources for the seven years Everett was at Cornell. Dr. Denis Condon's dissertation, *The Foundations of the Cornell School of Rhetoric*, was written under my direction at the University of Pittsburgh (1988) and has invaluable biographical information about other members of this influential group. For this information, I have borrowed shamelessly from Professor Condon. The other source is Raymond F. Howes who took undergraduate courses with Everett and completed his master's with Hoyt Hudson at the University of Pittsburgh. Howes is the unofficial chronicler of the Cornell School of Rhetoric and anyone who presumes to write about that subject must consult his various essays and sketches, most especially those collected in *Notes on the Cornell School of Rhetoric*. In addition, our correspondence over the years and his help with my previously published essay on Hudson gave me an even better feel for that period than anything else.

My decision to skip lightly over Everett's tenure as Dean at Swarthmore was not lightly taken. As mentioned before, I believe his official activities properly belong to a history of Swarthmore and his personal relations belong to the memories of those he helped. For Hunt's view of those days, his own book, *The Revolt of the College Intellectual*, remains the best source. There are a number of histories of Swarthmore during these years that I consulted, and they are mentioned in the footnotes.

For his retirement years, I relied primarily upon our correspondence, and my memories and notes from visits to Swarthmore. Professor Harold Barrett was kind enough to send me materials about Hunt's western tour in 1969 including an audio recording of his speech, "The Rhetoric of Violence."

Acknowledgments

I am appreciative to a variety of organizations and people who have helped in the preparation of this book. The Speech Communication Association commissioned it and gave permission to quote extensively from Hunt's articles that appeared in the *Quarterly Journal of Speech*. In this matter and others, Dr. James L. Gaudino, Executive Director, and Dr. James Chesebro, Director of Education Services, extended even more helpful service than a member has a right to expect from the busy officers of a professional education association.

President Clark Kerr of Berkeley took time from his schedule to talk about his days as a debater at Swarthmore. Professor Wilbur Samuel Howell was kind enough to write a brief description of his experiences as an undergraduate in a course with Hunt at Cornell University. Professor Lester Thonssen sent letters that were helpful about Huron College and South Dakota, and Mr. Eugene M. Lang sent copies of his remarks at Everett's ninety-first birthday celebration at Swarthmore. Each of these made contributions to helping me present Everett Hunt and his writings to the reader.

Various librarians at Cornell, Swarthmore, and the University of Pittsburgh helped in more ways than can be recounted here.

But it is to Everett and his family that I am most indebted. In addition to being a warm friend, Everett sent me long autobiographical letters and unpublished pieces that he had written. The most important of these autobiographical letters with a four page, single-spaced letter written on April 5, 1968. He left his papers to me and among them were additional autobiographical materials.

Alan Hunt kindly read the manuscript not with an eye to censorship but for the purpose of correcting various factual errors that I originally committed. His patient readings and wise guidance, especially about matters of which I have no personal knowledge, were of invaluable assistance. Since I did not know Dorothy Rossman Hunt, Everett's first wife and Alan's mother, I have relied almost exclusively on Alan for the brief comments about her. Surely these are inadequate, but a description of their remarkably happy marriage and her role in helping Everett fulfill his responsibilities as Dean of Swarthmore are matters I feel are beyond my scope and abilities.

Finally, I am indebted to Marjorie Hunt, Everett's second wife, whom I did know. She was a charming hostess during my many visits to Swarthmore both while Everett was alive and after he died. She urged me to write a biography of Everett as a rhetorician, turned his letters and papers over to me, and gave complete permission to quote from all his writings, including his letters, both published and unpublished. In addition, she provided a variety of details about his years in retirement that I would not have had access to otherwise. My greatest regret is that she died before this manuscript was completed.

Even as I thank the people who have assisted in the preparation of this book, I alone bear responsibility for its contents. In some small measure I hope it pays tribute to Everett Lee Hunt and causes one or two people to go back to his published writings to encounter a remarkable man who was both intellectual and humanist, a friend of ideas, but more a friend of people.

Theodore Otto Windt, Jr.
Pittsburgh, Pennsylvania
July 30, 1990

1

Sketch of a Friendship

At the Speech Communication Convention panel honoring Everett Lee Hunt on his retirement in 1959, C. Harold King remarked: "We all know the cliches about teachers. They are patient; they are selfless beings who devote themselves to the welfare of youth; they are self-effacing, not claiming their just due; they are secular saints, without compensation of halos. I regret to inform you that all of these bromides apply to this man, Hunt."[1] These comments about Everett Lee Hunt were indeed true. He was distressingly normal. And yet . . . .

No one could ask a question or make a comment about ideas quite the way Everett could. No one could correct an upstart young scholar with such reasonableness as Everett. No one could gently prod a friend along the way and give hints for which way to go the way Everett could. But it was all in the originality of his comment, in the succinctness of his question, in the sweet reasonableness of his attitude, in the prod or the hint. Rarely would Everett "open up" to say fully what he thought about an issue or an event. He preferred to write out his thoughts in the essay or formal speech rather than speak them extemporaneously. But always there was an originality, a freshness that provoked a thousand thoughts in his listener or reader.

That's the way I remember Everett.

I first met Everett on September 20, 1963. I remember the date well because it was two days after my first son was born. I had come to Temple University from Ohio State University where I had completed all my course work toward a doctorate in rhetoric and theatre. Before I left Columbus, my adviser, Harold F. Harding, gave me a copy of a letter of introduction to Everett Hunt that he had sent. "He will be expecting you to call upon him once you're settled in Philadelphia," Hal informed me.

Quite frankly, I was surprised to learn that Hunt was still alive. Like other graduate students of that time, I had read Hunt's "Plato and Aristotle on Rhetoric and Rhetoricians." Because of its mature scholarship and the fact that it had been published in 1925, I assumed its author must have been long since dead. I was surprised to learn that Hunt was not only alive but had just recently retired from Swarthmore College. Not knowing much about the East, I was delighted to learn that Swarthmore was a suburb of Philadelphia. Hal urged me to contact Hunt when I arrived in Philadelphia, and I assured Hal I would as soon as I was settled.

But once in Philadelphia and trying both to get acclimated to my first teaching job and prepared for my son's birth, I had little time to think about calling Hunt. I must admit also that I was apprehensive about calling him, even with Hal's letter of introduction. After all, I had not even completed my dissertation, and Hunt was a very famous man in our profession. In addition, I had only lately begun studying rhetoric. I had gotten my B.A. degree in English, my M.A. in Theatre, and had originally gone to Ohio State to continue my studies in Theatre. After a year and a half, I changed over to Rhetoric. In other words, I still felt uneasy about being a novice in my own professional field, and the idea of visiting with a prominent scholar of Hunt's stature unnerved me.

However, celebrating a bit more than I should have the night my son was born gave me an inflated sense of courage. And so, in mid-evening, I drew upon that artificial courage and called Everett Lee Hunt. He promptly invited me to Swarthmore two days hence.

I took the train from Philadelphia for the thirty minute ride out to Swarthmore and was met at the station by Everett. He was not at all what I expected of a scholar at an elite Eastern school. He was a relatively short man (about 5'8") but with a vigor that belied his age. He had touches of the broad midwestern twang to his voice and an equally broad smile to go with it. He wore a brown corduroy jacket over a plaid flannel shirt with a western string tie. He put me at ease by greeting me warmly as if I were an extremely important guest come to visit. That ease quickly changed when he began to drive us over various curbs, sidewalks, and lawns during the three block trip to his home. How he ever manuevered the car into his narrow driveway mystifies me even today. It was only after we settled into lawn chairs in his backyard that I began to regain my composure.

I had prepared a long list of terribly serious scholarly questions about classical rhetoric to ask Everett. But my preparation was futile. He was more interested in asking than answering questions. Everett asked about my dissertation which I—being young and in the midst of completing it—was all too eager to pontificate about. When I did attempt to ask a question, Everett turned my questions into questions of his own. And again, I got on my soapbox to tell him all manner of profound things that I thought about classical rhetoric, Plato's philosophy, the state of American-Soviet relations, and so on and on. But above all, he wanted to know about where I came from, what schools I had attended, what I wanted to do with myself both personally and in the field of rhetoric. His interest was not intrusive, but genuine.

On the few occasions that he actually answered a question, I noticed that he paused to put his thoughts into careful order. Once composed, he flicked his eyebrows upward and complete sentences rolled off his lips. But his expression remained placid.

Let me give an example from a conversation I recorded a few years later. This excerpt may illustrate both Everett's style and his reflective cast of mind. It was during the height of the criticism of the Johnson administration's policies in Vietnam. And one of the less hysterical charges at that time was that Johnson's rhetoric did not correspond with the realities of Vietnam. I asked him what he thought of that charge. After long thought, he replied:

> The statement that Johnson's rhetoric does not correspond with reality seems to assume that it would be perfectly possible to have a rhetoric that did correspond to reality. But this...seems to assume that it is very simple to comprehend and define reality.
>
> Johnson probably wants to achieve certain ends that he thinks are essential for the prosperity of the United States in its relations with other nations of the world, and he uses those arguments which appeal to him.
>
> Critics may say he is not giving a correct account of the facts, that he is not considering the various types of audiences that he has.
>
> But I suspect that if any person made speeches over the whole country, as Senator Fulbright and others are doing urging a completely different war policy, it would be debatable that their rhetoric would come any closer to reality than Johnson's rhetoric.
>
> If rhetoric is the faculty of discovering all the available means of persuasion, it seems to me that it's rather difficult to accuse anyone of not corresponding to reality. If that were a simple matter, then it would seem that debates and rhetorical discussions would not continue as indefinitely as they do.
>
> It is impossible to establish what reality is.
>
> If one takes the Platonic Ideal that reality is ideally located in the heavens above and that rhetoric is the faculty of persuading the different types of souls of the truth of that divine reality, then this [determining reality] would be simple.
>
> But if one genuinely believes that communism, for example, is an overwhelming threat to the world and must be stopped within its own borders and that if we allow it to spread we are suffering great danger for our own people, that seems to me to be a pretty realistic rhetoric from Johnson's point of view.

If you take another point of view that [of] the so-called "domino theory" of communism—that one country falls after another until it [communism] becomes the dominant power—and [you believe] that this theory is false and that communism tends to divide itself as it has done in China and in Russia and that there is no need in fearing that expansion of communism, then of course our whole attempt to stop it in Vietnam seems like an absurd and ridiculous attempt totally out of touch with reality.

And so the reality in question becomes what is the fact about the communist menace?

It seems to me that sometimes intellectuals feel they are in touch with reality in ways that merely practical men are not. And I would say that the statement that Johnson's rhetoric is out of touch with reality is itself a highly rhetorical statement.[2]

Everett Lee Hunt

Such answers were typical. But let me return to this first visit.

When occasionally I pressed him with more questions on a point, he would reply that he had been retired for several years and before that he had been in administration for twenty years. He would shake his head and say he was hopelessly out of touch with current scholarship. Clearly he preferred to ask questions rather than answer them.

As my first visit with him wore on, he said he greatly appreciated me taking time off to come to Swarthmore and help him do a little catching up. And that meant another round of questions.

Around 4 p.m. it was time for me to go. To my great relief, Everett suggested that we walk over to the train station. His wife would be coming in from teaching music in Philadelphia, and he said they liked to walk back after she arrived. So, we set off down Princeton Avenue to the end of the block, followed the fence line that separated the railroad tracks from the field behind the high school to the train platform. It was a walk that I was to make many times over the next twenty years.

On the train back to center city, I felt embarrassed that I had talked so much. I had gone to Swarthmore to pick his mind, and he picked mine instead. I thought I had made a fool of myself, and had it been physiologically possible, I would have kicked myself all the way back to Philadelphia. I thought of Sherwood Anderson's short story, "I Am a Fool," and felt an excruciating kinship with the central character.

But those feelings began to fade two days later when I received a letter from Everett saying how much he enjoyed my visit and inviting me to come again soon. And I felt fully at ease a month later—at the annual Pennsylvania Speech Association convention—when he mentioned my dissertation study of Khrushchev in the same breath with Marie Hochmuth Nichols and Karl Wallace as examples of scholarship that weds rhetoric and politics in a humane way.

Soon thereafter, I took him up on the invitation to visit him again and thus began a twenty year friendship. For the first five years I always addressed him as Dean Hunt until a letter arrived that began: "If you don't mind calling me Everett it might encourage an illusion of youth that I need badly."[3] And so it was Everett from then on.

Typical of our talks during these visits was our disagreement over the Free Speech Battle of Berkeley. I took the side of Mario Savio and the Free Speech Movement. As a veteran of the Ohio State free speech battle, I was absolutely convinced that the FSM was right and the Berkeley administration was not only wrong but malevolent as well. Savio's speech, "An End to History," had been very important in helping me understand what had happened at Ohio State as well as Berkeley.

Everett readily agreed about the importance of the principle of free speech, but he noted that there might be something to the administration's case. He said he had recently received a letter from one of his former debaters, Clark Kerr, (then President of the University of California system) explaining the difficulties he encountered in trying to deal with the FSM on the one hand, and civil authorities on the other. He said it was Kerr's opinion that the battle wasn't over freedom of speech at all, but over political action on campus, something the university rules prohibited. "It's not an easy time to be an administrator," he noted.

Our discussion then reminded him of a prank Kerr pulled when he was a student at Swarthmore. For commencement with all sorts of dignitaries in attendance and on the dais, including members of the Clothier family (of Strawbridge and Clothier) who were strong financial backers of the college, Kerr and some fellow students hung a huge "Lit Brothers" sign from Clothier Tower. But that was long ago. "Today's students seem so serious, I wonder what they do for amusement."

Although Everett's gentle reminder that there might be another side to the issue had little effect on my opinion of the issues, his anecdote gave a human face, even an adolescent one, to an administrator I had only thought of in the political stereotypes of the times. I learned a little lesson that day about easy stereotypes and one-sided, cliche thinking.

That was in 1964 and only the first glimpse I had of Everett's extensive correspondence and friendships around the country. But it was also typical of the way he expressed his opinions. As I later learned, he felt much greater sympathy (one of his favorite words) for administrators than student protesters. Given that he had spent the last 20 years of his career in administration that is understandable. Yet, I never heard him condemn protesters, even after the tragic death of President Courtney Smith of Swarthmore in 1969, with anything approaching the moral outrage of others. (In fact, Clark Kerr did not have a high opinion of Everett's book, *The Revolt of the College Intellectual*, because he thought Everett was inflating their importance by calling such protesters, "intellectuals.") Instead of condemning people, he would only remark about the sadness of events.

In 1965 I left Temple to accept a summer visiting teaching job at Bowling Green State University before going on to a new teaching appointment at the University of Texas in El Paso. At Bowling Green, Professor Ray Yeager organized a conference that summer on "Rhetoric and the Modern World." Everett journeyed by train from Swarthmore to the conference and delivered the keynote address, "General Specialists: Fifty Years Later."[4] It was then fifty years after the founding of the National Association of Academic Teachers of Public Speaking, and Everett used the occasion to reflect on the changes in the profession over those years. But it was the touches of autobiography that he included in his address that sparked my interest in writing about him and his contribution to the profession.

Once in El Paso, that interest began to form into more concrete plans. The Department of Speech and Theatre had a strong connection to Cornell University in Gifford Wingate, the chair, who had received his doctorate from Cornell. A year later Hal Harding left Ohio State to join us as H.Y. Benedict Professor of Rhetoric, and James Wood who was completing his degree at Cornell joined us as well. Soon, one of Everett's former students, John H. Powell, left the snows of Iowa for the desert of West Texas to become a visiting professor of History and an enthusiastic friend and guide. Hal secured a contract from Southern Illinois University Press for me to edit a collection of Everett's essays for its "Landmarks in Speech" series. And I began gathering material for the introductory essay. Everett sent long letters detailing his life (as he remembered it from the vantage point of age 77). I travelled to Swarthmore in the summer of 1967 to talk with him and to tape record his reminiscences. Hal contributed thoughts about his relations with Everett and his importance in the field. Jack Powell encouraged the project and gave me invaluable impressions of Everett at Swarthmore. Even though he was dying and feverishly trying to complete his last book (which was published shortly before his death under the title, *George Washington and the Jack Ass*), Jack took time to write a long section about Swarthmore that I later condensed and used in my essay about Everett. He also offered stylistic improvements throughout. (I always felt embarrassed that I had used one paragraph exactly as Jack wrote it, even though Jack insisted that I not credit him for it. Jack called them "improvements." That embarrassment eased somewhat when I read one of Everett's late essays and saw that Jack had "improved" two entire paragraphs in it.)

The book did not work out. It was not the fault of Southern Illinois Press, but my own. Not the least of these problems was a four year writing block. In addition, I got caught up in the political turmoil of those days. But finally in 1972, long after leaving El Paso, "Everett Lee Hunt on Rhetoric" appeared in *The Speech Teacher*. My failure to produce the volume of Everett's essays was off-set by his appreciation for the essay. In one letter he wrote:

> I still return occasionally and egotistically to your academic obituary of me, and am more and more impressed with what a thoughtful job you did. I am quite content to let my career rest with it. I have come to realize the truth of some of your observations that had escaped me earlier. In you[r] footnote on p. 184 you say 'Hunt misjudged the reaction of many men to industrialization and specialized labor.' You are entirely right. I realize now that my introverted values will always be esteemed by a small minority. A neighbor of [mine] who has recently retired...comes over to fix my car...and I realize that his ecstacy in putting a nut in place is stronger than my most poetic ecstacy. I realize again the truth of Wm. James' statements that men's values are determined by their interests, and that I should not expect to speak for more than a small minority, and perhaps mostly for myself. But I still have some hopes that a small minority may strengthen each other.[5]

Such sentiments were small but appreciated recompense for my feelings of letting him down by not completing the book.

When I returned to Pennsylvania in 1968 to teach at the University of Pittsburgh, I began going over to Swarthmore to visit at least once each year.

Gradually, I became an unofficial member of the family. Despite the almost fifty years in the differences in our ages, we found that we had much in common. Both of us came from the West (Everett from South Dakota and I from Texas). Both of us had entered small denominational colleges in preparation for the ministry (Everett at Huron College and I at Texas Lutheran). Both of us would readily admit that much of our thinking was founded on religious rather than secular beliefs. Both of us had switched to other interests during college and had prepared for teaching careers in one discipline (Everett in Rhetoric and I in Theatre) only to find ourselves eventually teaching something entirely different (Everett teaching English and I teaching political rhetoric). We shared a love of the West, church hymns, the Wisdom literature of the Bible (particularly Ecclesiastes), Ireland and Irish poets (especially Yeats' early non-mystical poems), and above all, owning our own homes. After I scraped enough money together to buy my first (and only) house in 1974, I rarely received a letter from Everett without some mention or question about it. Typical of the notes in letters was one he wrote a year before he died: "I have recently dug from my files the pictures of your rural home on Cabin Lane. You too can contemplate nature from your own windows. But I fear you are now too busy to do that. But when you reach my years you may well find your greatest satisfaction in giving thanks for 'the beauty of the earth and the wonder of the skies.'"[6] Everett had not owned his own home until his retirement and marriage to Marjorie. He was so proud of his home that on one occasion I would make a rush trip to Swarthmore at his request to discuss whether he should leave it or not. I shall presently get to that story.

But there were also some differences in addition to that of our ages. Everett had little use for T.S. Eliot's poetry ("too pessimistic," he would say, about the early poems and "too much influenced by his conversion to Catholicism" in the later ones) whereas I greatly admired all of Eliot's poetry. In fact, Everett had little use for either unrestrained optimism or unqualified pessimism. Everett had an almost Buddhist serenity about life that sorely conflicted with my own hot impatience about matters of even little import. Everett always put a greater stress on human cooperation than I. He had come from a political tradition of prairie socialism and the service tradition of the Quakers whereas I had been reared in an idiosyncratic form of Texas anarchism and in a highly personal form of Lutheranism. Everett had evolved from an ardent socialist into an equally ardent Democrat whereas my anarchist tendencies would evolve into an idealistic cynicism. In his later years, he had switched his intellectual allegiance from Isocrates to Plato and found in him a comfortable philosophic view of life for himself. But my "old dead Greek" hero was Diogenes with his lantern and his tub. Above all, Everett had spent much of his career as an administrator and therefore had considerable sympathy for the plight of college officials during the "troubles" of the 1960s and 70s. I was just beginning my career as a teacher and was inclined to look upon administrators (and indeed, authority in general) more with suspicion than sympathy. But it was both our common heritages and our comradely differences that matured into a close and loving friendship.

Everett did everything he could to encourage my writing (especially that work that did not involve specialized scholarship) and my career. What he did for me, I later learned, was only what he had done for hundreds before me. And I recount my personal experiences and appreciations as an example of the appreciation so many other must have felt. Everett kept up a steady stream of letters and began to introduce me to some of the people that he knew. Often this would take the form of him serving as go-between; at other times, I would hear from them directly.

A typical example was a phone call I got out of the blue from James Humes. For his Christmas present in 1982 Everett's brother-in-law gave him a copy of Humes' book, *Churchill: Speaker of the Century*. Hunt so enjoyed it that he wrote Humes who happened to reside in Philadelphia. Shortly thereafter I received a call one morning at my office from Humes. It seemed that he was preparing a book on speeches by each of the presidents, and Everett had told him I was some kind of authority on presidential rhetoric. He quickly found out that my studies were limited to the modern presidency and that I could be of no help whatsoever to deciding which speech by Polk or Fillmore ought to be included in his work. Once that was out of the way, Mr. Humes began to tell me about Churchill's speeches and even began to recite excerpts from them with an uncanny ability to mimic Churchill's cadences and voice. Our conversation was an altogether delightful surprise, but one that I should have become accustomed to from acquaintances of Everett's. I met even more people during my frequent visits to Swarthmore, including a neighbor who taught acting and was ecstatic to learn that I had seen him perform one of the "leads" in the Alley Theatre's production of *Waiting for Godot* in Houston back in 1960 . His excitement was so great that it became the conversational centerpiece of the little party the Hunts had arranged that afternoon and for which the Hunts had invited him. And both Everett and Marjorie were enchanted that their neighbor so enjoyed himself.

Each visit to Swarthmore had a ritual to it. Everett would, if possible, meet me at the station, and we would walk back to his 221 N. Princeton. Once I got my luggage settled into his study which was transformed into a guest room, we would retire to the living room, unless it was summer and then we would lounge in lawn chairs in the backyard. We would catch up on what each of us had been doing since my last visit. Everett would usually have several books that he had read since my last visit, either books he had mentioned or ones that I recommended in our correspondence. As soon as we got caught up, we would begin discussing those books and a myriad of other educational and personal matters. Rarely would we discuss articles or books by professional scholars in rhetoric and communication. Everett found the journals too technical for his tastes and most professional scholars too specialized and limited to gain his attention for any length of time.

Around 4 we would walk over to meet Marjorie Hunt at the train station. Marjorie and her sister, Helen who lived with them, would serve cocktails at 5 followed by a light meal after the MacNeil-Lehrer Report. Each evening Everett would do 500 turns on his exercise bicycle before bedtime, while I read something among the books in his library.

Each morning began with Everett taking a long walk (always before I was up) and then reading of the *New York Times*. By the time I was down for breakfast, he was anxious to discuss the news of the day. And we would talk all morning.

After lunch he always took a short nap and then we swam (in the summer) in an unseasonably cold pond or took a hike around Swarthmore College which he loved and never ceased to want to share with visitors. As we walked, he would be reminded of different events or people from the past. For example, we were standing one day in front of main college building looking down the long spacious tree-lined mall with its white wooden lawn chairs. He was reminded of the mother of an applicant that he had shown around the campus. As she looked down the mall, she said: "My son will absolutely love it here. This is just like his front lawn at home." At 4 we would once again walk over to the train station to meet Mrs. Hunt.

I tried to visit on week-ends. And to avoid imposing too greatly upon Everett and Marjorie, I usually sought to combine the visit with one to Ralph and Carol Towne in Philadelphia, whose inexhaustible capacity for hospitality rivalled even that of the Hunts. Frequently, Ralph and Carol would drive me out to Swarthmore and all of us would be able to visit together. For such occasions Everett, Marjorie, and Helen sought to provide some special entertainment. It might be a small cocktail party with friends or a reception with neighbors (such as the one already mentioned) or something personally special for me. Several of these bear mention.

One of these little entertainments still warms me with a special glow. In 1973 I used my sabbatical to spend two months in Ireland. Everett always had a place in his heart for Ireland because he had spent a semester studying at Trinity and lived next door to two of Yeats' sisters. He had even met W.B., the great man himself, at the Abbey Theatre. On one of my trips to Swarthmore, Everett told me he had prepared something special for the first evening. After the news and dinner, all of us retired to the parlor where Marjorie had her grand piano for the private music lessons she sometimes gave in her home. Helen and I seated ourselves as Everett announced he had prepared an evening of Irish music for me. With Marjorie

Everett and Marjorie

playing, Everett sang in that wonderful tenor of his a selection of more than a dozen Irish ballads and songs. The program continued for more than an hour with long and sustained applause from the two in his audience. I don't know who was more delighted—Everett or me—with the success of the evening.

But some visits did not begin so enjoyably. In 1979 I began to get a series of agitated letters from Everett. He was feeling his mortality. He had quit driving his car (Thank God!) and was beginning to put his books and papers in order to donate them to the Friends Library at Swarthmore or to dispose of them otherwise. But these changes did not account for tone of urgency that pervaded his letters. That tone was very uncharacteristic.

He eventually wrote about what was bothering him. Someone had suggested that at his age (he was 89) he ought to consider leaving his house and entering a nursing home. The idea of leaving his one and only real home horrified him more than the thought of going into a nursing facility. He began to write me about this possibility and asked for my advice. Since I was not a formal member of the family, I did not think it appropriate for me to advise him. I ignored his question and wrote instead about other matters. But his letters became more pointed on the issue. (Apparently, he did not talk to anyone else about it. Marjorie later told me she knew nothing about any talk of a nursing home.)

Finally, Everett asked me if I could come over as soon as possible to discuss what he should do. I quickly made arrangements for the trip, but I was uneasy about what advice I should give. So, I called Ralph Towne to tell him that I was coming to Philadelphia once again and explained the situation to him. I asked if he would go to Swarthmore with me to help in giving advice. As usual, Ralph readily agreed.

I flew to Philadelphia, spent the night with Ralph and Carol, and then the two of us drove out to Swarthmore the next afternoon. After a hour of conversational pleasantries on Everett's side porch, Everett obliquely brought up the nursing home. It was a moment I dreaded because Everett obviously was nervous about both the subject and what we might say. But Ralph saved the day. We solved the problem with great dispatch.

Once Everett broached the subject, Ralph quickly (and even a bit brusquely) asked: "Do you want to go into a nursing home?"

"No," Everett replied.

"Then, don't!" Ralph advised.

And that was that.

The light came back into Everett's eyes, I sighed a great relief and thanked my lucky stars for Ralph's directness, and we turned to other topics for the remainder of the afternoon.

My last visit with Everett came in the fall before he died. There was an elegiac quality to it. He had declined perceptibly. Instead of meeting me at the train station, he waited for me on the sidewalk in front of his house. In his later years, he sometimes walked with a cane. Now, he leaned heavily upon it. We had the usual warm greetings and evening conversation, but the next day when we began our hike around Swarthmore, Everett could no longer walk with his former vigor. He could go about 100 feet and then had to rest. Typical of him, he announced forthrightly that he tired easily. His angina. Would I mind stopping occasionally, he asked? I soon fell into the rhythm by finding something new about the campus (one I had come to know so well over the years) to attract enough attention for us to pause and remark about it. We slowly wound our way around the dogwoods and shrubs that make Swarthmore world famous for its landscaping and horticulture. Finally, Everett spied the destination he seemed to have had in mind all the while.

Would I mind sitting for a while, he asked, under that old sycamore tree? As we sat, Everett began to reminisce. I remember this last long conversation well, even though I sat on an anthill. (The following is in part reconstructed from an earlier letter Everett wrote me about his decision to come to Swarthmore.)

"I sat under this tree in 1925 trying to decide whether I wanted to leave Ithaca and come to this little village and Quaker college out in the country. Aydelotte and his committee met over in that building [pointing] deciding whether they would hire me. I came down here at Hoyt Hudson's recommendation. He had replaced Paul Pearson, but now was moving on to his real interests in poetry and criticism in the

English Department at the University of Pittsburgh. And then he went on to Princeton and Stanford and his distinguished career."

"The Public Speaking Department was the biggest department in the college, with strong alumni support because Pearson gave his students summer jobs in his Chautauqua. So, I sat here trying to make a very hard decision. I didn't have a doctorate and had no chance of getting one at Cornell which meant I had no chance of advancement there either. But I loved the Finger Lakes and the long walks around Ithaca."

"They offered me the job and a good salary and the possibility of getting my doctorate at the University of Pennsylvania. So I sat here trying to make up my mind. Finally, I decided and left Ithaca for this small country village."

"But four years after I arrived, Aydelotte Oxfordized Swarthmore for honors work and abolished speech. I didn't get my doctorate, and became a Dean instead and never did any more scholarship."

He paused for a long while and then concluded: "But the human relations and friendships here at Swarthmore more than made up for all that."

I don't think there was a time when I loved Everett more than during that half hour or so when we sat under the sycamore (now known as "Everett's Tree") and he talked about himself with the honest self-reflections that I had so long admired.

After a while, we got up, and I tried to brush the ants away without Everett noticing. We walked a bit more and finally made our way back to Princeton Avenue.

It was my last visit with Everett.

On May 2, 1984 Ralph Towne called me to say Everett had died two days before. Marjorie hadn't been able to get in touch with me because my phone number was unlisted. The cremation had been private, but a memorial service was to be held a week later. Marjorie wanted me to be there. Ralph once again generously offered to put me up the day before the service and said he and Carol would drive me out for it.

The night before the service Marjorie called me at Ralph's and asked me to speak for the family the next day. I was totally unprepared to do so, but assured her I would.

At the Quaker service the next day, I took my place with the others on one of the hard benches facing those who had gathered to pay their respects. On one side of me was Daniel Hoffman, the poet and critic, and on the other an elderly man whose hearing aid occasionally broke the silence with a shrill whistle. As is the custom with Friends, people rose to speak as the inner light guided them. I can't say an inner light moved me, but at some point during the service I rose and stammered out a few words about Everett's place in the Speech Communication profession. I added a few other words about my friendship with him and closed with the only words I could think of, a quotation from William Saroyan's preface to *The Time of Your Life*: "In the time of your life, live—so that in that wondrous time you shall not add to the misery and sorrow of the world, but shall smile to the infinite delight and mystery of it."

Two weeks later, during the break between our winter teaching term and the beginning of the summer term, I returned to Swarthmore to help Marjorie and Helen dispose of Everett's books and papers. Marjorie had asked me to return and take charge of Everett's papers and correspondence and to help her decide what to do with the books remaining in his library. Most of his books had been donated to the Friends Library at Swarthmore or to the library at Huron College, but there were some left that needed to be disposed of. I found a few that I would like to have, and Marjorie generously told me to take what I wanted. I picked out a few others to send to young scholars who had formed friendships with Everett in his last years. I thought they might like to have them too.

But there was one book that I put aside for Ralph Towne and gave to him when he came out at the end of the week to gather me up once again. It was a book that in his later years Everett rarely failed to mention when I visited, one that he had read more than once because, he said, it reminded him of the ideal he had set for himself. The book was John Gross' *The Rise and Fall of the Man of Letters* with the subtitle, *A Study of the Idiosyncratic and the Humane in Modern Literature*. Everett Lee Hunt was a man of letters and his rise within his profession was due to his idiosyncratic and humane commitment to that ideal. And in the end, it was only death that felled him, not the vision he maintained throughout his life. Instead, that vision sustained and nurtured him as well as all those who came in friendly contact with him.

Notes

[1] C. Harold King, "This Man, Hunt," paper read by Carroll C. Arnold at panel honoring Everett Lee Hunt, December 28, 1959.

[2] Taped interview with Hunt, August 10, 1967.

[3] Letter from Hunt to Windt, April 5, 1965.

[4] Posthumously published in *Rhetoric Society Quarterly, 17* (Spring 1987), pp. 167-176.

[5] Letter from Hunt to Windt, June 14, 1973.

[6] Letter from Hunt to Windt, May 17, 1983.

2

Early Prairie Days

Everett Lee Hunt was born October 14, 1890 in Colfax, Iowa to Charles Reeve Hunt, a peripatetic Presbyterian minister and sometimes schoolmaster, and his wife, Anna Belle. A daughter, Olive, was born two years later, but lived only two weeks. In 1898 another daughter, Genevieve, was born. His father, originally an Indiana Quaker, attended Wheaton College and turned Presbyterian in order to become a professional minister. Then as now, ministers move from call to call and the Hunts were different only in the many times they moved. (Hunt could remember at least ten different times, ranging as far south as Deming, New Mexico and as far north as the small towns of South Dakota between his birth and when he was thirteen.) The reason for these moves was that the Rev. Hunt was what the Presbyterians call a "home missionary." His responsibility was to establish new Sunday Schools and new schools in hopes of creating Presbyterian churches in sparsely populated areas of the country.

By 1899 they had moved from Iowa to the small hamlet of Mt. Vernon in the hills and hollers of southeastern Kentucky. There his father ministered to his flock and presided over a school, the Mt. Vernon Collegiate Institute, for poor mountain whites.[1] He also served as president of Alexander College in Burkesville. Everett's recollections of those days were of trips with his father through the mountains to interest mountaineers in coming to a school in an area "where the predominant influence was that of prosperous farmers and raisers of fine horses along the banks of the Cumberland River."[2]

Of his boyhood days in Kentucky, Everett had two especially fond memories. First, the frisky youth got in trouble with the authorities. Ever fond of horseback riding, he once rode too dashingly through the town square and was arrested and fined by the local sheriff for riding at a "gallup, not a gait." Also, he met his "first love," Luana Whitehead, about whom he remained very sentimental: "[I] have written her every Christmas to say 'Skeeters am a hummin' on the honeysuckle vine, Sleep Kentucky Babe."[3] The occasion in 1981 for writing about Ms. Whitehead was a letter Everett had received from Professor Tracy of Southwestern Louisiana. Professor Tracy had delivered a scholarly paper at the Pittsburgh Symposium in honor of Everett, and Everett had written each participant in appreciation. Tracy answered by noting that his department chair was the son of Luana Whitehead, "your most intimate boyhood acquaintance." In his letter to me about this correspondence, Everett concluded: "Academic life has no thrill for me equal to this."[4]

From Kentucky, the Hunts moved to South Dakota where they resided in a series of small towns. His father was responsible for organizing Sunday Schools in the territory beyond the Missouri River to the Black Hills. He travelled the area with a spring wagon, a team of ponies, a folding organ, stopping wherever there seemed to be a new settlement that might support a Sunday School in hopes of someday building a church there. In one of them, Meadow, they built and lived in a sod house[5] of which Everett was quite proud in his later years. After a brief period in New Mexico, the family came north again, this time to Fountain City, Indiana. Everett attended public schools for two years, and it was here that he first learned about his Quaker heritage from his grandparents. The stay was longer than some others, but the family soon moved back to the wilds of South Dakota and in Huron —a "city" of little more than 3,000 souls—when Everett was 13.

His life as a minister's son in our fortieth state left a lasting impression on him. The land was harsh and life was hard. The battle of Little Bighorn had been fought about 25 years before (in 1876), and the territories (Montana, Wyoming and the Dakotas) were fully opened only after the final war at Wounded Knee. The gold rush had brought speculators and settlers, but the drought and depression at the end of the century withered the population.

Life was indeed harsh on the lonesome prairies. But it quickly taught people the virtues of banding together to face common adversity. The Christian home and church were centers of Everett's life. The family conducted daily Bible readings and prayers. These instilled in him religious habits of thought, especially that habit of seeing life as whole and purposeful. In one of his early essays, he lamented that students often did not realize that "we live in a universe instead of a multiverse."[6] His search for unity amid diversity, for larger purposes to life in a world that often gave little thought to much beyond private interests would become central themes for both his professional and personal life. Although he did not wear his religion on his sleeve, as the saying goes, Everett's Christian beliefs—first Presbyterian and later those of the Religious Society of Friends—profoundly influenced his approach to his teaching, writing, and living.

It was also at this time that Everett began his life-long love for music, a persistent passion of his life. In one of his later letters he remarked:

> In my father's Presbyterian church I memorized so many hymns that they have stayed with me and deeply move me, whatever my intellectual convictions. Even our Quakers now go back to hymn singing, and sing twice a month for a half an hour before the Meeting for Worship. Some, of course, stay away. My wife, Dorothy, helped edit the first *Hymnal for Friends*, and included many old timers, such as "Faith of Our Fathers."
>
> When I was a sophomore in College I sang in a minstrel show. Afterward the director of the Presbyterian quartet choir came to me and said she needed a tenor for her quartet for a concert dedicating a new organ, and her tenor had just moved away. If I would take his place she would give me singing lessons free of charge. I did this for four years and when the director moved away I became choir director, with Dorothy Rossman, my future wife, as accompanist. That brought us together. I have continued singing all my life, and still sing every night while the girls [Marjorie Hunt, his second wife, and her sister, Helen Watson] are washing dishes, often including hymns—also many folk songs, plus Brahms, Schubert, Schumann, etc. I love the music and the poetry of the songs equally, and the evening of poetry is an inspiration far beyond that of scholarship.[7]

Music was such a passion with him that when he made his first trip to New York in 1916 to attend his first professional meeting of the National Association of Teachers of Public Speaking, he was uncertain whether he was more thrilled by being invited to speak at that meeting or by the opportunity to hear Caruso at Carnegie Hall. Needless to say, he did both. But that is getting a bit ahead of our story.

College Days

In 1908 Everett entered Huron College, which the Presbyterians had founded in 1883. It had gone through several name changes. Originally, it had been called the Presbyterian University of Southern Dakota but was quickly renamed Pierre University in honor of the town in which it was first located. The citizens of Pierre offered 20 acres of land for the school and $13,000 to get it started. The original campus consisted of one wooden building located on a bluff known as "Rattlesnake Hill" overlooking the muddy Missouri.[8]

But the college fell on hard times when the Dakota "boom" ended in the late 1890s. The Presbyterian Synod of South Dakota decided to move the college from Pierre to Huron in 1898 and to consolidate it with Scotland Academy, thus to provide both a preparatory or high school as well as a college. The name, of course, was changed from Pierre to Huron College.

By 1908 Huron college's enrollment was 40, the faculty numbered about 14, and some 70 courses were offered students. The college had not yet adopted the curriculum of more advanced, Eastern schools; had not yet instituted the electives system. The classics, which Hunt majored in, and Christian ideals constituted the core of a liberal education. His college transcript reveals that he took 5 courses in Greek and 7 in Latin (somehow taking "Sophomore Latin" the year *before* he studied "Elementary Latin." This may be explained by the fact that he had previously had two years of both Greek and Latin at the Academy.) Nothing comparable to the electives now available to students appears on his transcript. Instead, there are traditional courses in Rhetoric and Composition, Algebra, Solid Geometry, English History, Chemistry and Biology, and a series of courses in Principles and History of Education.

As befitted a church-related college, the curriculum was heavy with courses in the *Bible*, including two semester courses in both The Gospels and The Epistles, as well as others in [Christian Ethics and Apologetics]. There was little doubt that the religious atmosphere permeated both the school and the curriculum. About this atmosphere Hunt later wrote:

> Huron College in its early days was dominated by a rather dogmatic Presbyterian ministry. In my day the local Presbyterian ministers forbade the installation of a pool table in the Y.M.C.A. room because students might later play the game in evil places. They also sought to remove an ordained minister from the faculty because his teaching was too liberal. Three of his four students who entered the Princeton Theological seminary soon abandoned the ministry and this was evidence that their Huron religious training had been too liberal.[9]

In his freshman year, Hunt described this atmosphere in a gently satiric piece called "Chronicles," written in scriptural phraseology and which I shall begin at the fourth verse:

> 4. It came to pass that certain ones of the young shepherd lads did those things which were evil in the sight of the faculty.
> 5. Therefore when the wise men were reasoning together among themselves (in a faculty meeting).
> 6. One of them arose and lifted up his voice and cried unto them saying,
> 7. Behold, now, many of the young shepherd lads and the maidens do us not honor, as is seemly,
> 8. But they mock at us, and make merry; yea, they study not, neither do they recite.
> 9. But we receive shekels for putting words of wisdom into their mouths.
> 10. Therefore let us make a decree that they may do those things which seem good to us.
> 11. And they all shouted with one accord and said, it seemeth good to us!
> 12. Wherefore they said unto Thomas (who was one of the wise men, a keeper of books)
> 13. Lo now, thou shalt watch over that room in which the young men and the maidens are wont to come together to seek wisdom.
> 14. And thou shalt keep guard over it, lest they move their stools in divers parts of the chamber.
> 15. Or talk together in an unseemly manner, or cast missiles at each other.
> 16. For these things do we hate, yea, one more thing is an abomination unto us,
> 17. That the young men should idle with the maidens.
> 18. Therefore, Oh Thomas, do thou see that they do none of these things.
> 19. And Thomas saith unto them, All these things which ye have commanded me will I do (and then some).[10]

Huron could not have been as oppressively fundamentalist as Everett contended because these "Chronicles" were "read in the chapel at an open meeting of the Philomathians [the College Literary Society." However, he did note rather ruefully that the reading "caused Sam Van Voorhis to threaten to beat the head of the guy that wrote it."[11]

During his five years in college (he missed a semester due to illness), Hunt was a whirlwind of activity. He ran the College bookstore, joined practically every literary organization, served as junior class president, sang in the glee club, acted in plays, and in his senior year edited the college newspaper, *The Alphomega*. He did not participate in collegiate athletics because he was born with club feet, which later exempted him from service in World War I. But he made up for this by becoming a well-known horseman and vigorous walker. *The Rubaiyat* described him in 1912 as being "one of the most energetic fellows you ever saw, and may be observed taking a 5 a.m. stroll to the Jim River, 'slinging hash' at the 'Northwestern,' going to class six steps at a time, or pounding the Editorial typewriter." It also noted that he "had made himself notorious within recent months by superseding Lundberg as the local exponent of Socialism."[12]

Among his close friends were the Hudson brothers. "There were four Hudson boys, Hoyt, Clough, Ray, and a fourth whose name I cannot remember. They formed an athletic team and challenged the rest of the college and always won. It was the father's heart condition that led him to fear that intercollegiate athletics would impose more heart strain and thus he forbade them to take part."[13] Like Hunt, they were sons of a fundamentalist minister. Clough Hudson had been born the same year as Hunt and was the first editor of the *Alphomega*, but it was Hoyt Hudson, three years younger, who became a life-long friend of Everett's.

Pictures in the yearbook show Hoyt Hudson as an extremely handsome young man with a diffident air about him. Often the pictures show him slouching with his head turned aside as if he were contemplating some private vision. These pictures are quite in contrast to the full-faced photographs of Everett with his straight-forward open face. The 1911 *Rubaiyat* described Hudson in this way: "Some men are born great, some achieve greatness and some have greatness thrust upon them, but seldom does one find a man who is a happy combination of these three conditions. Hoyt H. Hudson, however, comes in this class. There is no sphere of activity in which he does not feel perfectly at home. His sudden and unexpected flights into the realms of the poetic, his oratorical spasms, his argumentative nature, and his extemporaneous work in the class room all mark him as a precocious genius." It also noted that he was a "general favorite both with the students and with the Committee on College Absences."[14] Although he was 3 years younger than Hunt, he would graduate a year before him and wander off to various points in the midwest and western states until Hunt summoned him to complete his graduate work at Cornell University. Together they would be instrumental in laying the foundation for the Cornell School of Rhetoric. Their close friendship would last until Hudson's untimely death in 1945.

As an undergraduate Hunt distinguished himself as a fearsome debater. "I majored in Greek and Latin because my father had done so in his preparation for the ministry, but I had not the least expectation that it was a specialized training for a career. My real enthusiasm was for debating, and especially debating both sides of a question."[15] Debating was not the narrow academic enterprize that it is these days when the audience usually consists of one judge who is a debate coach from another school. At the turn of the century when few forms of entertainment reached out to the great plains of America, college debates were singular events that combined the intellectual and the entertaining into a major civic event. The public attended the debates and local newspapers wrote up the results. One example may demonstrate the high esteem in which these events were held.

On April 22, 1912 the Huron College team journeyed to Brookings to debate the team from State College. An 11 inch by 14 inch pink poster announced the debate for that evening in the college auditorium and the question: "Resolved That Constitutionality Aside The Principle of The Recall of Judges Should be Adopted by The Several States." Pictures of the debaters appeared on the poster. For the Huron team: Arnold Bliss, Albert Sheldon, and Everett Hunt; for the State College team: Harry Rilling, Henry White, and Perry Clifford. At the top in bold print was the tease: "Do You Believe in The Recall of Judges." At the bottom of the poster was the notice that a 35 cent admission would be charged.

The debate was a furious one, closely contested. The Huron *Morning Herald* told part of the story the next day in a news report entitled "A Unanimous Decision" with the subtitle "To Huron in Debate with Brookings. Everett Hunt for Huron Team is largely responsible for the victory." The reporter wrote:

> The Huron College Debating team [that debated the negative side], consisting of Bliss, Sheldon, and Hunt was given a unanimous decision over the team from Brookings consisting of

Messrs. Clifford, White, and Rilling, which upheld the affirmative. The teams were both strong in the presentation of their constructive argument, and it was undoubtedly Huron's work in rebuttal which prompted the judges to render their decision in their favor. In this respect Everett Hunt, the last speaker for Huron, both in constructive argument and in rebuttal easily excelled any other member of either team. Speaking from no set speech it is not too much to say that his clear thought and masterful delivery won the debate for Huron.[16]

The Brookings *Industrial-Collegian* agreed: "Hunt is certainly a whirlwind in rebuttal."[17] And the *Daily Huronite* noted: "Huron's victory was due to the excellent manner in which the three speakers assembled their facts, and to the really powerful rebuttal by Everett Hunt, who in the few minutes allowed him rounded out his case and refuted the assertions of the affirmative so completely that there was no possibility of the decision being otherwise than in the negative's favor."[18]

At this time, a victory in debate was as glorious an event as a football victory. When the debaters returned from Brookings, they were met at the train station by a large crowd with a team of horses and a wagon to haul the debaters through the town and back to the college for a bonfire celebration. But some football players, jealous of this honor, unscrewed the cap that held a wheel to the wagon, and the wheel fell off. Some in the crowd pushed the wheel back on. When they could not find the cap, they pushed it back on at every turn, all the way back to the campus bonfire, where an even larger crowd gave college yells for the resounding victory at State College.[19]

In addition to his debating prowess he also gained some repute as an orator. His oration, "The Home-Made Child," won second place at the Kent contest and was printed on the front page of the *Alphomega* on March 21, 1913.

During his collegiate career Everett Hunt developed as the premier debater from Huron. At the end of the school year of 1913 *The Alphomega* noted:

For four years he has upheld the honor of the school by his work in argumentation and his ability is such that he is feared by every rival team in the state. Mr. Hunt's style of speaking is not showy or bombastic; but quiet, forceful, and convincing. He has the ability to take instant advantage of every misstatement of his opponents, and his rebuttals have become famous for their keenness and irrefutable force. Three times he has opposed Yankton and each time he has demonstrated that he is a dangerous opponent in both constructive and destructive argument. It is with regret that we see him pass from the debating team by graduation.[20]

But he was not passing from the debating team, only graduating from a debater to debate coach and to a new career as teacher of public speaking.

Public Speaking at Huron

Due to a shortage of teachers during his senior year, Hunt was drafted to teach a Latin course in Cicero. Upon graduation he was appointed Instructor in Latin, Oratory, and Debate, later described simply as Public Speaking.

In its short history Huron College had developed a rather extensive program in public speaking and, as it was called, "expression." The school was proud of the tradition it was creating. The official history of the College noted that in 1899, Walter Hubbard, one of the four "original" students who formed the first class at the newly named College, won first place with an oration on Wendell Phillips in the interstate oratorical competition in Wahpeton, North Dakota. The whole town celebrated by having not one parade in his honor, but *two*.[21]

By the next year, 1900, the College had created a School of Oratory and Expression and hired Elbert R. Moses as Instructor in Oratory and Physical Culture for Men. It was the beginning of a period of speech education (from 1883 to 1911) that Donald W. Rasmussen called the "period of elocution and oratory."[22]

It should be remembered that few colleges or universities offered courses in public speaking. Speech was conceived as expression or elocution and taught primarily in private schools or by private teachers. When colleges offered courses in public speaking, the instruction was usually in elocution and generally located within English Departments. Indeed, the place of public speaking as a "poor relation" to English and Composition would become the major reason for the separation of speech from English in 1914 when finally the National Association of Academic Teachers of Public Speaking was formed.[23] Prior to the formation of the National Association, college level instruction was largely at the whim or intelligence of whoever was chosen to teach such courses. Thus, idiosyncratic approaches characterized the wide range of offerings not only among various colleges and universities, but within the colleges themselves. As one teacher left and another took over, the course offerings could change just as dramatically and as rapidly. Huron College was no exception.

As mentioned already, the first instructor at Huron was Elbert Moses. The official purpose of the School of Oratory was "to train those who wish to become proficient in the various lines of dramatic art."[24] To this end, six semesters in Physical Culture were offered along with two semesters in Vocal Culture, three in Elocution, another in Pronunciation, and three in Oratory. The work in Physical Culture was work in light gymnastics.

In 1903 Grace Isabelle Little came from the Emerson College of Oratory and brought the Emerson system with her. This system of elocution created by Charles Wesley Emerson stressed the evolutionary development of expression through four stages: The Colossal Period, the Attractive or Melodramatic Period, the Realistic Period, and the Suggestive Period. All of this was covered in the first year while the second year was devoted to "The Sixteen Perfective Laws of Art."[25] In addition to these courses, a variety of extracurricular activities in speech, including debates, theatrical performances, readings, oratorical contests were sponsored and carried on not only by the School of Oratory, but by various collegiate literary societies as well. The Emerson system continued to be the core of the program until the School was abolished in favor of a Department of Dramatic Art and Public Speaking. Much of this change must have been due to the arrival of a new professor of public speaking on campus.

In 1911 Dr. Charles Kimball Hoyt joined the faculty and set public speaking on a different course in his two short years at the College. He had been trained at Hamilton College, a school with a rich history of instruction in speech. Dr. Hoyt set about adding new courses to the curriculum including three years of instruction in public speaking. In addition, he secured college credit for participation in intercollegiate debate and enlarged the forensic program. He spoke frequently and vigorously at Chapel meetings urging greater support for the forensic program.[26] He was widely admired during his brief tenure. The 1911 *Rubaiyat* described him as one who had "lifted the ideals and broadened the view of his students in ethics, oratory and literature" and stated that he had "surpassed even the excellent reputation which preceded his entrance upon his work here last fall."[27] His star debater, as we have already seen, was Everett Hunt, who was soon to succeed him.

Hunt's First Teaching Appointment

When Dr. Hoyt retired at the end of the 1912-1913 school year, the new President of the College, Harry M. Gage, appointed Everett Hunt as Instructor in Latin, Oratory and Debate with what Everett described as "a minimum of anything like technical training" for the job.[28] To compensate for his lack of training, Hunt journeyed to Chicago in the summer of 1913 to take private lessons in oral reading and speaking from A.E. Phillips, a private teacher.

Arthur Edward Phillips (1867-1932) was an Englishman who had emigrated first to Toronto, Ontario and then to Chicago which he made his home for the remainder of his life.[29] He taught at the Lutheran Theological Seminary, managed his own tutoring service for business and professional people, lectured widely in and around Chicago, and wrote popular articles on public questions as well as textbooks on speaking. He was a member of the National Association of Elocutionists (later the National Association of Academic Teachers of Public Speaking) and was a leader in the movement to change the word *elocution* to *speech* (which occurred in 1906 when the association's name was changed to The National Association for the Advancement of Speech Arts). He read widely in the classics, in contemporary psychology and public speaking. Karl Wallace described his book, *Effective Speaking* (first published in 1908) as a "logical, practical, beautifully clear theory of speech composition."[30] Over the years the book sold more than 75,000 copies. Everett spent the summer studying with him and later would use his book as a text in his public speaking courses. Hunt also took private singing lessons at the Cosmopolitan School of Music and sang in the University of Chicago Choir under the direction of Robert Waterman Stevens.

Upon his return, he began to reshape the curriculum and extracurricular activities to his own preferences and interests. His background in the classics provided him with a very different model of what public speaking ought to be, one thoroughly grounded in rhetoric rather than elocution. His interest in current affairs, undoubtedly motivated by his experience in debate, gave substance to his courses. In his 1915 "Teacher's Report" he explained his emphasis on contemporary themes and issues because "very few courses in the college curriculum do creative work upon present day themes."[31] The changes foreshadowed the arguments Hunt would soon make in pressing for the primacy of substance over form and his insistence that teachers of public speaking concentrate on current issues.

In the school year 1914-1915 Rasmussen listed the following courses in public speaking from the college catalog:

Professor Hunt, Huron College

> *Expression*—A course in the use of voice and action in speaking and reading. Texts: Curry's *Imagination and the Dramatic Instinct*, Phillips' *Natural Drills with Selections*, and Curry's *Province of Expression*.
> *Argumentation*—A study of the principles of debating. Analysis of propositions and brief-drawing are given particular attention. Occasional debates on current questions are held. Text: Foster's *Argumentation and Debate*.
> *Oratory 1*—An elementary course in the principles of effective speaking. Special emphasis laid upon the construction of speeches. Ability to think before an audience will be cultivated. Text: Phillips' *Effective Speaking*.
> *Oratory 2*—The aim of this course is to produce sound thinking and clear, correct, and effective oral expression of the thought. Subjects are assigned in the field of literature, art, science, and politics. The writing of the oration is studied. No text.
> *Oratory 3*—A course in the preparation of various types of public addresses. Methods of gathering material discussed. Subjects for orations are brought before the class. Reading in current periodical literature is assigned. The aim of this course is to furnish ideas for effective speeches. No text.[32]

The following year some of these courses had their titles changed. Some were compressed into a single course. And a new course that bore Hunt's distinctive signature was offered:

Political Speaking—Political Oratory of America studied. Issues that have been prominent in the history of the nation are discussed from the viewpoint of the men who spoke upon them. Debates upon current issues. Living orators studied. Course especially designed for students desirous of entering public service.[33]

One can see the unique approach Hunt was taking. On his own (and perhaps through the influence of Dr. Hoyt and Hunt's own experience as a debater), he changed the curriculum from one that stressed elocution to one that stressed debate and speaking on public issues.

In an early essay, Hunt described how he went about teaching his courses:

My first meeting with [students in Public Speaking] is usually a written quiz—a general information test, an inquiry as to their interests outside of required studies, and as to their reading habits. Periodical reading is usually the first thing I emphasize and insist on. I hold them to account for a knowledge of the *Atlantic*, *The North American Review*, the *Nation*, *Literary Digest*, and *Current Opinion*. In order that they may not read them with a feeling that they have done their whole duty in so doing, I assign many special articles in various other periodicals. I have them report on these, without notes.[34]

Hunt stated that he thought it of greater importance "to make an undergraduate want to make a speech than to tell him how to make it" and that "the acquiring of any new intellectual interest is of equal importance with improvement in formal argumentation."[35]

Hunt later said he hardly gave any instruction in speech techniques or the methods of making a speech, but rather taught "the subject matter of their [students'] speeches. If they got an interesting idea and talked interestingly about it, that was sufficient for me and I didn't worry much about it."[36] Instead, he continually urged students to read essays and articles about ideas, especially about current events or timeless contentious issues, such as the Great Man theory of history.

He had little use for the text books, few that they were, of the time. He noted that in his search for materials for his courses he was "led to the conclusion that the majority of books of selections published are a standing indictment of the good taste and literary knowledge of our profession." He was compelled, he said "to waste many valuable hours making my own books with a mimeograph and loose leaf notebooks."[37]

There was one exception. He stumbled upon a book entitled *Representative Essays in Modern Thought* edited by Harrison R. Steeves of Columbia University and Frank H. Ristine of Hamilton College. The book, published in 1913, contained some 19 essays ranging from Matthew Arnold's "Sweetness and Light" to William James' "The Moral Equivalent of War." This volume was profoundly influential on Hunt. A decade later his book, *Persistent Questions in Public Discussion*, would be modelled on it. Furthermore, the Introduction to *Representative Essays* contained a credo that coincided with Hunt's beliefs: "This book has been compiled under the conviction that composition can be taught more effectively with ideas rather than with literary models or set exercises as the point of the departure."[38] Later, Hunt recalled that when he read the justification for teaching ideas rather than rules, he said that was for him. That's what he wanted to do. *Representative Essays* also contained an outline of a two term course of teaching composition which Hunt adapted to teaching public speaking. The book undoubtedly became a point of departure for Hunt. From that time on, he would use such an approach in his quest for raising public speaking to a respectable level by making public speaking subject-centered.

Even though Everett was a one person department and taught all the courses in speech, he maintained and expanded an already heavy schedule of debates. He arranged for more intercollegiate contests, organized a Women's debating league, created interclass debates between freshmen and sophomore debaters with both men's and women's teams. He prepared an issue of the 1914 Huron *Bulletin* that was devoted entirely to educational opportunities in speech and sent it to high school students throughout the state to attract them to Huron College. For the 1916-1917 season, he prepared brochure that folded out into three 3 by 5 inch panels. Pictures of the debate team of that year (including Emil Utterback who later followed Hunt to Cornell for graduate work and years later would be one of my professors at Ohio State University) and of Hunt were on one side of the three panels. The back sides had one panel announcing the First Annual Forensic Bulletin for the year accompanied by a picture of Huron College and another panel listed the contests for the year. As Rasmussen noted: "During Professor Hunt's years as director of Huron College speech there was a constant stream of publicity concerning the department. In most of this, debate was given the greatest emphasis."[39] He was so successful that at the opening of the 1916 school year, 25 students answered the call for candidates in debate, a number representing more than 20 per cent of the entire student body.[40]

During these years Everett seemed to be at the center of both academic activity at the College and entertainment in the town. In addition to staging debates and directing plays, Hunt formed the Huron College Concert Company consisting of himself as tenor, Ms. Lola Alley, soprano, and his sister, Genevieve as pianist. The small brochure which had a picture of the three members of the company on the front announced they were available for "a limited number of engagements in South Dakota during the 1916-1917 season." Another small brochure had its front page filled with a very dramatic photograph of Hunt and an announcement that he also was filling a limited number of engagements for dramatic readings that season. It cited a review from the *Daily Huronite* about a previous public reading of Stephen Phillip's *Paolo and Francesca*: "The reading was given in a masterful manner, the characters of the play being brought before the audience as clearly as though they had appeared in costume on the stage. The high praise which was accorded Mr. Hunt last night shows that the residents of Huron are anxious to hear more of his work." One of the things I remember most vividly about Everett in later years was that whenever he began to read aloud, his voice took on an entirely different tone and manner—much more dramatic and emphatic—than when he was engaging in casual conversation. The break between conversation and reading was sharp and unmistakable. Listening, as I have been while writing this, to the recording of his seminar at Temple University in 1971, I hear that distinctive change as he moved from talking about a subject to reading from some essay or article that he had brought with him.

As he began his career, Hunt had also begun to form his ideas about who he was as a professor and what ought to be taught in courses in public speaking. Every novice teacher faces this problem. Teaching is a learning process for the teacher as well as the student, learning not only one's material, but learning who one is as a teacher. It's a delicate process, and takes a lot of rehearsing to find one's comfortable self in the classroom. It cannot be stressed too emphatically that Hunt and other teachers of public speaking at this time were often working in isolation from one another. And for one lodged in a tiny sectarian school in the wilds of South Dakota that isolation was even more poignant. He did not have a clear model of what a teacher of public speaking was supposed to be. *Representative Essays* had made its imprint upon him as a guide to what to teach. But that still did not answer the question of what kind of teacher he would be.

Hunt later recalled that at about this time he read an article by Bliss Perry entitled "The Amateur Spirit." It was an article that was to have lasting influence on him. Perry had divided his time between the academic and literary worlds and moved easily back and forth between the two. He taught at Williams, Princeton, and Harvard and for ten years edited the *Atlantic Monthly*.[41] Perry eschewed professionalism in academe and exalted the intellectual amateur who could roam over various fields of knowledge with no special claim to expertise other than his own inquiring and imaginative mind as a guide. The amateur "works for love, and not for money," and cultivates an art or a study because "he is attached to it, not because it gives him a living, but because it ministers to his life."[42] Such a person, Perry believed, would not be constricted to any specific field of study, but would feel equally at home in any intellectual activity. Perry concluded about this amateur:

> The highest service of the educated man in our democratic society demands of him breadth of interest as well as depth of technical research. It requires unquenched ardor for the best things, spontaneous delight in the play of mind and character, a many-sided responsiveness that shall keep a man from hardening into a mere high-geared machine. It is these qualities that perfect a

liberal education and complete a man's usefulness to his generation. Taken by themselves, they fit him primarily for living, rather than for getting a living.[43]

Reading these words early in his career made an indelible impression on Hunt. Henceforth, he would be that educated amateur and live his life in accordance with its ideals. Anyone who would presume to understand Everett Hunt's life could do no worse than begin by reading "The Amateur Spirit."

Later in 1935 Perry authored a book of reminiscences called *And Gladly Teach* that Everett admired greatly for its gentle humor and warm humanism. But it was the "amateur spirit" that captured his imagination. And throughout his career Hunt would persistently deny he was a professional *anything* in preference for calling himself an amateur, which is usually defined as "one who follows a pursuit without proficiency or a professional purpose."[44] It could hardly be said that Everett lacked proficiency in rhetoric, but it might be said that he pursued his teaching of rhetoric with a personal rather than a professional purpose. But he also meant he was an amateur in its older meaning—as a "lover" (from the Latin *amator*), a lover of debate, of language, of all things human and interesting.

First Forays into Professional Activity

Huron College was, one might justly imagine, somewhat remote from the "mainstream of American life." But it was undoubtedly a college, and the young instructor was encouraged to pursue his academic interests. (Everett probably was introduced to professional activities through A.E. Phillips who had been active in the preceding professional organizations. Later in life Hunt would say that he missed out on being one of the founders of the profession by a year.)

In 1914 a small group of teachers of public speaking broke away from English and formed the National Association of Academic Teachers of Public Speaking, now called the Speech Communication Association. These teachers created the Association to signal their separation from departments of English and from the dominance of elocution. To give themselves a distinct professional identity, they turned to major questions about what directions teaching and research in public speaking ought to take, about how their new academic departments ought to be organized, about goals for the organization and its members. These issues were argued at annual conventions and in the first pages of *The Quarterly Journal of Public Speaking*, the new professional organ of the organization that began publication in 1915 under the editorship of James M. O'Neill. O'Neill, the most vocal advocate of separation of public speaking from departments of English, also served as first president of the Association.

The first issue of the journal carried two articles that sparked Hunt's debating spirit. In "The Need for Research," James Winans of Cornell University asserted that scientific research into various aspects of speaking was need to establish public speaking as a respectable member of the academic community. He called for scientific studies that would advance knowledge in public speaking in a way comparable to the advances made in medicine and economics.[45] In the second article, "Research in Public Speaking," the newly formed Research Committee of the National Association maintained, "Some academic subjects have arisen as pure sciences and later been applied to the practical problems of life. Public Speaking has come by the other road, having been first a practical or semi-practical subject and then aspiring to become more like a pure science."[46] Research, the report concluded, would produce technically trained teachers for the profession and thus was urgently needed.

Everett Lee Hunt—a 25 year old instructor at an obscure college in South Dakota with two years teaching experience under his belt, a young man with only a B.A. degree in classics and a few private lessons in public speaking—raised his voice in opposition. His first essay, "Debating and College Advertizing," gained him entry to the profession. His second, "The Scientific Spirit in Public Speaking," was sent to the editor and set off a vigorous controversy within the new profession when it was published in the second issue of the new journal.

Hunt wrote that public speaking is more akin to literature than physics. Thus, it should not be studied as a technical, specialized science. He did not object, he said from his lofty perch in Huron, to research which would dispel misconceptions about public speaking, but he feared that excessive specialization and scholasticism would minimize the human element in speaking and be "as fatal to enthusiasm and inspiration in public speaking as they have been to broad and sympathetic development in many of those branches [of learning] where they now prevail.",[47] He feared that technical research would become a goal in itself, and would eventually replace teaching and learning as the principal force in academics. In voicing these fears, he struck a note that was to become his theme as teacher and writer: "May we never substitute imitation for originality. May we never exalt learning above sincerity, academic recognition above service, or logic above life."[48]

Hunt soon found himself engaged in a series of debates with leading members of the National Association, among them Charles H. Woolbert, a prominent figure in the movement to separate speech from English. Woolbert, who later received his doctorate in psychology from Harvard, outlined a Department of Speech Science (as he would have the new departments called), which he clearly intended to serve as a prototype. Research and teaching in this department would include: Phonology, Techniques of Expression, Psychology of Expression, Application of Laws of Express, The Acting Drama, Extempore Speaking Argumentation and Debate, Persuasion, Pedagogy of Oral Expression, Aesthetics of Speaking.[49]

The debate was joined when Hunt's "General Specialists" and Woolbert's "A Problem in Pragmatism," a rebuttal to Hunt which editor O'Neill commissioned him to write, were published in the same issue of the *Quarterly Journal*.

Hunt wrote that the Department of Speech Science envisioned by Woolbert "gives rise to the conception that the technique of a speech can be successfully abstracted from the subject matter and formalized; whereas it is a truism that you cannot separate the style from the man."[50] He urged that speaking not be placed in the laboratory. Techniques cannot be so easily separated from ideas. Instead of a scientific department, Hunt advocated a department of "general specialists":

The Public Speaking department is to serve as a clearing house of ideas. The instructor should inspire in his students a vital interest in the affairs of the world, in politics, sociology, economics, literature, and art. He must realize with Cicero that all the arts which pertain to culture, have as it were, a common bond; and he should make his students realize it. Too many students are graduating without the slightest realization of the relationship of the various departments in which they have worked. They have no vivid sense that we live in a universe instead of a multiverse. To the question, 'Has't any philosophy in thee?' they can only reply with a stare.[51]

Hunt called teachers of speech to return to the intellectual ideal of the nineteenth-century college president who could occupy any chair in a college. He saw departments of public speaking fulfilling the need for men and women of general culture who would bind together the fragments of knowledge specialists create.[52]

In his reply Woolbert remarked that he and Hunt shared no common ground on this issue:

Charles H. Woolbert

Mr. Hunt and I are of different epochs and countries. He is of a romantic golden age, I, of the common, ignoble now. He is from Greece, I am from Germany (!)—he probably by choice, I perforce. He cries out for the glory that was Greece and the grandeur that was Rome; I am surrounded by laboratories and card catalogues.[53]

Woolbert went on to describe Hunt as "a sort of lay pastor, an intellectual and spiritual knight errant, an educational court physician."[54] Such characteristics belong properly to college teachers where they are appreciated, but they are, Woolbert implied, inappropriate and impractical for university professors. Research and specialization are required in universities, and teachers of speech, if they wish acceptance by colleagues, must adapt to these standards. Woolbert maintained that speech should be studied as a distinct discipline—a field whose content should be carefully detailed analysis, experimentation, identification and description of effective speaking techniques.[55] "I stand for a search for the facts; the facts of how speaking is done; of what its various effects are under specified conditions; how these facts can be made into laws and principles," he wrote.[56] He believed that the only means for discovering these facts lay in scientifically conducted investigations and research.

Everett's early essays prompted an invitation for him to speak at the 1916 convention of the National Association in New York. It was his first trip East. The contrast between Hunt and the new leaders of the Association must have been as startling as it was stark. James Winans was 44 and a full professor of Public Speaking at Cornell. Charles Woolbert was 39, had taught at Albion College, the University of Illinois, and was preparing to begin his doctoral work at Harvard the next year. James M. O'Neill was 35, had done graduate work at Harvard, had taught at Dartmouth, and recently had been appointed head of the new Department of Speech at the University of Wisconsin. And here was Everett Hunt—a very young instructor of barely 26 with only a B.A. degree from an obscure church college in South Dakota and who had taught for less than three years—questioning the coalescing conventional wisdom of his elders.

Years later, he mused over his audacity in daring to challenge such preeminent people. And when he was asked how he got the courage to jump into these debates—even more than that, Hunt created the debates—he gave a variety of answers. He always seemed a bit embarrassed about his impudence and would say that he just liked to write and these issues interested him. Or he would say he liked the competition of debate, and once it got started, he enjoyed these exchanges. More often than not, he would merely shake his head at his own audacity, chuckle about it, and remark that the others must have found him and his ideas "silly." At the Temple Conference he recalled that he had no sense of professionalism, nor did he ever want to be a professional at anything. At Huron College, no one had really cared what he taught, he said, as long as he met his classes and performed his duties as debate coach. As noted previously, he had read Bliss Perry's "The Amateur Spirit" and had adopted it as his credo. He wanted to wander in his own amateurish way among ideas that interested him.

In his 1916 address to the national meeting he described such people as himself as one of those "autumn loiters," taking that description from Browning's poem "Paracelsus":

And men have oft grown old among their books
To die, case-hardened in their ignorance . . . .
While, contrary, it has chanced some idle day
That autumn loiterers just as fancy free
As midges in the sun, have oft given vent
To truth.

He added, of course, that he did not believe that such people would ever "solve many problems in the psychology of Public Speaking," but he thought them to be as important as experts in psychology. (These gentle barbs were obviously aimed at Woolbert whose passion was the psychology of speech.)

But such answers about his entry and participation in these early debates are too modest, even though they probably were sincere reasons for his original articles. More to the point, Everett Hunt truly believed that specialization and scientism were antithetical to creative teaching. These themes became the consistent themes of both his career in education and in his life. And when he walked into the lion's den in New York a year after the founding of the National Association, he pressed them in his own humanistic way.

Hunt entitled his address, "Academic Public Speaking." The speech was divided into two parts: (1) a defense of his ideas against the attack from Woolbert in "A Problem in Pragmatism"; and (2) a brief exposition of what he taught in his courses at Huron College. He began by saying:

> Professor Woolbert . . . almost dealt a death blow to all my ambitions by declaring that I am not modern. I belong to the age of Greece and Rome he says. It is a terrible thing not to be modern. It is almost the worst thing that could be said about a man. But I recall Bernard Shaw's remark about Ruskin. It was easy, he says, for Ruskin to declare that it is better to die than to do an unjust act, for dying is a very simple matter; but when it comes to determining what justice is, there is a difficulty.[57]

So too, Hunt continued, it "is easy to condemn a man for not being modern, but to determine what it is to be modern, that is another matter."[58] Everett went on to repeat his arguments against specialization and to call for a place for the "autumn loiters" who teach by example rather than by precept. After explaining how he taught his courses at Huron, he concluded that: "it seems to me to be greater to make an undergraduate want to make a speech than to tell him how to make it."

In his address, Hunt did make attempts to demonstrate that he too was concerned about the practical matter at hand, that is, gaining a respectable place for public speaking in colleges and universities. But his attempts in these areas were again tied to the issue of specialization, and his belief that teachers would gain their place and recognition by a "voluntary association with men and books," rather than through intensive research.

His argument was not persuasive. Woolbert's immediate rejoinder playfully predicted that in the future Hunt would achieve fame through research and experimentation.[59]

The disagreement between Hunt and Woolbert (and the many others who sided with Woolbert) transcended methodology and pedagogical techniques. Each in his own way defined public speaking within the context of American colleges and universities. Woolbert's concern was that speech be accepted as a separate and responsible academic department. He recognized that prestige was accorded scientific studies and urged scholars in speech to conduct scientific research. He saw specialization proliferating among other academic departments and urged that teachers of speech specialize. "I can only say that in an age of organization and specialization I am for specializing and organizing," He wrote, "where techniques is demanded, I yield to it if I can do so without sin . . . ."[60] He was confident that when speech was conscientiously studied as a technical field clearly distinguished from other fields, it would take its equal place in the university. In comparing the career of Woolbert to Winans', who also studied psychology of speech, Carroll Arnold concluded: "We are the poorer . . . because Woolbert, the psychologist, did not, like Winans, the humanist, go on to erect an *art* of rhetoric on the theoretical base he so ably laid . . . ."[61] The critic must observe that Woolbert was not interested in rhetoric, but in the psychology of speech. His decision to isolate speech from the humanities and his concentration on technical studies probably prevented him from ever constructing an *art* of rhetoric. His vision was too limited; his concerns too immediate.

Hunt shared little of Woolbert's sense of urgency in developing public speaking as a technical department, nor was he overly concerned about creating a separate and distinct field of knowledge. He was more interested in larger questions that admitted of no final answers nor immediate imperatives. What interested Hunt were the effects of specialization on knowledge and about the service teachers of public speaking could perform in educating liberal students who would, in turn, be interested in service and ideas. He believed the plain purpose of a liberal education was to prepare young men and women to assume their public responsibilities. Teaching techniques without real concern for ideas or ideals undermined this goal because it ignored the unity among ideas and the differences among students. Hunt wrote: "The kind of students we as teachers of speech want in our classrooms are not plodding scientists, effeminate aesthetes, or scholastic prodigies. We want men who are to be leaders of men, who will have an active share in all public affairs."[62]

The goals proposed by Hunt comprised a far higher calling for the new profession than the curriculum of mechanics and techniques advocated by Woolbert. Public speaking courses, as Hunt viewed them, would necessarily draw heavily on information from other disciplines, and thus, by implication, assert a unity among diverse areas of knowledge. Consequently, students and teachers would have to leap over the boundaries Woolbert strove to place around speech. Specialization would not serve or be served.

The problem was that Hunt could not or would not develop a system or curriculum or theory to put his ideas into practice. That was the very thing the profession needed at that time. But Hunt, always the gadfly, was too skeptical of easy generalizations, too wary of regimented theories, too fond of debating ideas to be concerned about working out a specific, practical curriculum. Moreover, he was never certain that the study of speech or rhetoric constituted a profession, and he persisted in calling himself an amateur. Even more to the point, he did not realize the politics of establishing a new discipline within a university. Hunt's ideas might serve as an inspiration to individual teachers, but they would hardly persuade a hard-pressed Dean to grant money and facilities for a new Department.

Professionalism and specialization, as Woolbert correctly noted, were the emerging standards of the day, both in academic life and in cultural life.[63] Thus, Everett Hunt impressed some of his hearers as a bright young man with a bright future, but his address left his hearers unconvinced.

These early debates and experiences formed lasting ideas in Hunt about teaching, public speaking, scholarship, and the profession. From thenceforth for better or for worse, he would identify academic scholarship with a "search for the facts" and would find that uninteresting to him. "Scientism" or "scholasticism" he would call these searches. And he would find such academic work less rewarding and less worthy than the pursuit of general ideas of continuous controversy. He would make a clear distinction between specialized studies written for other academics and his own rambling among general ideas of common interest to intellectuals or the literate public. The former he would look upon with a wary eye; the latter would spark his undivided attention and interest. He would have no feel for professionalism even as he would make distinguished contributions to the profession. He would do so in his own amateurish way out of love for his subjects and his urge to write about whatever interested him.

But Hunt had his sights on an even greater problem, one that transcended academic and professional concerns. He saw not only knowledge fragmenting, but modern American life as well. The old order of the nineteenth century had passed away, but a new order for a new century had not been created to replace it. The problem that Hunt was grappling with was one that a number of other intellectuals were also addressing in different ways. We might best understand this by digressing for a moment to consider what Walter Lippmann wrote about this problem more than a decade after Hunt began writing.

In 1929 Lippmann wrote *A Preface to Morals*. In it he confronted concerns similar to those Hunt addressed. About the problem of modernity, Lippmann wrote:

> For the modern man who has ceased to believe, without ceasing to be credulous, hangs, as it were, between heaven and earth, and is at rest nowhere. There is no theory of the meaning and value of events which he is compelled to accept, but he is none the less compelled to accept the events. There is no moral authority to which he must turn now, but there is coercion in opinions, fashions and fads. There is for him no inevitable purpose in the universe, but there are elaborate necessities, physical, political, economic. He does not feel himself to be an actor in a great and dramatic destiny, but he is subject to the massive powers of our civilization, forced to adopt their pace, bound to their routine, entangled in their conflicts. He can believe what he chooses about this civilization. He cannot, however, escape the compulsion of modern events. They compel his body and his senses as ruthlessly as ever did king or priest. They do not compel his mind. They have all the force of natural events, but not their majesty, all the tyrannical power

of ancient institutions, but none of their moral certainty. Events are there, and they overpower him. But they do not convince him that they have that dignity which inheres in that which is necessary and in the nature of things.[64]

Lippmann concluded that "Whirl is King having driven out Zeus."[65] A decade earlier Lippmann had made the same distinction as Hunt between those who see "government [and life] as a routine to be administered and those who regard it as a problem to be solved."[66] Now in 1929 Lippmann proposed a more encompassing solution. To deal with this new world in which certainty was lost, tradition ridiculed, and authority diminished (except when enforced by brute force), Lippmann sought to construct a new rational humanism that would be brought to bear as a guide in confronting the daily problems of living and the practical problems of governing in a democratic society.

Hunt shared Lippmann's view of these problems. In a world of science and specialization, Hunt would divide problems between those that scientists and experts could address and those that resided in the realm of probability. These latter problems would be his principal concerns. If belief could no longer be discovered in the nature of things and authority no longer had power to compel belief, he would find in public persuasion, in rhetoric, the method for attempting to address and resolve such problems. In this new world of uncertainty and probability, he sought to create a modern conception of rhetoric as the humanistic instrument for grappling with the great problems of government and morality as well as the daily problems of living. But he had less faith in reason than Lippmann. His humanism would be a rhetorical one, not a strictly rational humanism, but one based on sympathetic appeals to all of a person's senses, not merely to the mind. And he would grow increasingly skeptical about the power of reasonable persuasion to perform these tasks. Eventually, he would occasionally conclude that the only significant persuasion that actually takes place is self-persuasion.

Although these themes and his conception of rhetoric were only developed in a rudimentary way in these early essays, they were beginning to form the personal themes and conceptions that Hunt would consistently adapt and apply throughout his career to a variety of issues in a variety of settings, be they academic disputes, issues of literary or rhetorical criticism, administrative problems, or the confusions of bright undergraduate students. The seeds were planted in these initial forays into professional work, but at the time his attention was turned to other matters.

At the 1916 convention Hunt did make an personal impression. He was named to the committee to inquire into the teaching of homiletics in schools of theology. And he began to form friendships that would be lasting both personally and professionally. The first of these was with James Winans of Cornell University, who invited Hunt to give a guest lecture at Cornell the next year. When the war broke out and teachers were scarce, Winans offered Hunt a position in the Department of Public Speaking at Cornell. But he declined the initial offer. The second friendship was with Charles Woolbert himself. Although they disagreed vigorously, Hunt found Woolbert charming and willing to be helpful to the young instructor. They began a friendship that would last until Woolbert untimely and early death in 1929.

Final Days at Huron

When Hunt returned to Huron, he continued writing. His final essay from his Huron years, "An Adventure in Philosophy," was published. It was a typical Hunt article of this period—philosophic in perspective but "philosophy with a smile," as he called it quoting Renal. What Hunt attacked this time was the separate attempts by Woolbert and Mary Yost to find a single unity amid all the diversity in the profession as a theoretical approach to research and study in the new profession:

> Miss Yost proclaims that the real fundamentals are to be found in the field of sociology, and that distinctions not arising from the social situation are antiquated in oratory. And now Professor Woolbert, from his psychological laboratory, announces that 'since mental processes can be described and explained (I have yet to learn of anything 'explained' by science) only in terms of psychology,' the solution of the difficulty is to be found in psychology alone.[67]

In contrast to the sociological and psychological perspectives, Hunt wrote from the philosophic perspective. And that perspective, in Hunt's eyes, saw no such thing as fundamental, or at the very least that "any claim of any one branch of learning to be final or 'fundamental' should be very carefully examined."[68] The central and controlling idea of this rambling essay was what was becoming a distinctive mark of Hunt's thinking and writing: the direct questioning of any idea or theory that presumed to be all inclusive. Although Hunt persistently celebrated the unity of life, he was equally persistent in disclaiming that any substantive discipline or theory or idea could find or express that unity. Paradoxically, even as he pointed to anomalies, he insisted that people go beyond them to seek some higher principle at stake. In other words, he was skeptical of all-encompassing theories or ideas, but equally distressed about any claim of relativism to replace them. Thus, trying to pin down Hunt in the way in which other intellectuals or theorists can be catalogued or consigned to a particular school of thought is a fruitless and maddening task. "An Adventure in Philosophy" expressed this skepticism more than any other essay of this time.

This was the final essay from the Huron years, and the last in his debates with Woolbert about the direction of the profession. Now, his situation would change, and his career would take a very different turn.

By the fall of 1917 Hunt had grown restless. He had achieved a degree of stature in his profession as the result of his publications and papers at conventions. Being an ambitious young man, his glimpses of horizons beyond the plains and hills of South Dakota beckoned him to new worlds as yet unconquered.

More important, he had been deeply stung by Woolbert's description of his ideas and of him as being appropriate only to a college setting. Years later, he would recall Woolbert's description either in conversation or in one of his autobiographical writings. Even fifty or sixty years later, he could almost quote those biting words verbatim.

Little wonder that in those early days he felt academically inadequate, what with only a B.A. degree in Classics, while others had Masters or doctorates or were working toward them. What stature he had achieved was diminished by the fact that he possessed no advanced degree. In an age of specialization, the M.A. or Ph.D. conferred the proper credentials upon a teacher. It simply was not enough to have good ideas, even good ones that were published. He needed the instant respect that went with advanced degrees, the designation of "expert" that would give greater force to his ideas and would gain him the opportunities for advancement in his career.

A year before in 1916, he completed a correspondence course in philosophy, "Problems in Philosophy," from the University of Chicago. But trying to get a Master's by correspondence was a time-consuming task for an energetic young man who had already begun to make his mark. Attempting to get a doctorate in the same way was probably futile.

Therefore, in the late fall of 1917 (sometime in November or early December), Everett wrote Charles Woolbert to ask for advice. At this time, Woolbert was on a leave of absence from teaching to pursue graduate studies at Harvard in the Department of Philosophy and Psychology. On Christmas Day, 1917 Woolbert replied with a long typewritten letter written in a spirit of fatherly (or maybe older brotherly) advice.[69]

After traditional season's greetings, Woolbert expressed in no uncertain terms his reaction to Hunt's most recent publication: "I say to you without reserve that it has been many days since I have been as incensed as when I read that first paragraph of yours [in Hunt's "An Adventure in Philosophy"] with its gratuitous insult." After defending himself, Woolbert moved the his reason for replying to Hunt. He wrote that he was concerned about the welfare of the profession and Hunt's general usefulness in promoting the profession. To that end, Woolbert urged Hunt to leave Huron College (which "will never save your soul") and seek an advanced degree. Then, Woolbert launched into a long description of the "miracle that Harvard can work in a man" by opening the eyes of eager young students to the wise experience of teachers and "intellectual delights" of Harvard studies and associations.

Woolbert concluded the letter with appeals for Hunt to leave Huron and come to Harvard for graduate work. He even sent him the bulletin of the Department of Philosophy and Psychology and urged him to apply for a graduate scholarship or prize that would provide the financial support to allow him to do graduate work.

The letter was almost a turning point in Hunt's career. Despite their professional differences, Woolbert had generously offered sound advice to Hunt and had agreed to help him pursue an advanced degree at one of the most prestigious universities in the country. The possibility of going from Huron to Harvard was a mind-dazzling leap for Hunt, but Woolbert was willing to do whatever he could to help Hunt make it successfully. And Woolbert was as good as his words.

Hunt applied to the Department of Philosophy and Psychology for graduate work and was accepted. In the spring, Harvard appointed him as an Austin Scholar in Philosophy for 1918-1919. Huron College was justly proud. The April 10, 1918 issue of the *Alphomega* carried a front page story of the appointment and concluded: "Mr. Hunt's appointment not only bespeakes [*sic*] the success of his personal achievement but also those of his Alma Mater. It shows that Huron's graduates are fitted to attain distinction in the largest universities of the country."[70]

Hunt was elated. His passion had always been philosophy with a strong undercurrent of theology. And here he was all set to pursue his passion in one of the distinguished graduate departments in the country.

But, alas, it did not work out that way. Shortly after accepting the Harvard appointment, there was a family crisis. Hunt never described the specifics of the crisis, but apparently both his father and mother fell seriously ill and were unable to provide for the family. (His mother would die shortly after the family's arrival in Ithaca in 1918). The financial burden of providing for the entire family fell upon Everett, and it made going to Harvard with its small stipend impossible.

It so happened at this time that James Winans was taking one of his walks in the woods near the Cornell campus and happened to run into one of Hunt's friends from Huron who chanced to be walking in the same woods on the same day. They apparently fell into conversation during which Winans remarked about the difficulties he was having getting qualified teachers of public speaking due to the War. Hunt's friend spoke up and recommended Everett, but Winans said he had already been turned down because Hunt was going to Harvard to study philosophy. Hunt's friend assured Winans that those plans had changed and that Hunt was now available.

Winans subsequently wrote Hunt again offering him a position as Assistant Professor of Public Speaking at Cornell at the grand salary of $,000 a year, a munificent sum given Hunt's financial straits. This time Hunt had little choice but to accept. Leaving Huron behind, he moved his family to Ithaca to join a department that would make a major contribution to the history and development of public speaking in America. Nonetheless his financial condition was such that President Harry M. Gage of Huron had to lend him the money to move to Ithaca, an act of generosity that forever endeared Hunt not only to Gage but to Huron College itself.

The Huron days were over, but in a different way that Hunt had originally imagined. Instead of pursuing a degree in philosophy at Harvard, he would be teaching public speaking at Cornell. Instead of enrolling to take graduate courses, he would create the first graduate seminar in classical rhetoric in the United States in the twentieth century. Instead of a life devoted to philosophy, he would now play a major role in giving dignity and substance to the study of rhetoric.

Or so he would do at least for the next ten years.

Notes

[1] Letter from Hunt to Windt, September 1, 1981.

[2] Untitled manuscript, "dictated 3/8[19]56," p. 2.

[3] Letter from Hunt to Windt, September 1, 1981.

[4] *Ibid.*

[5] Sod houses had been a fixture on the great plains ever since settlers first moved West. Since these arid plains often had no trees, pioneers used the buffalo or bluestem grass with its tough matted roots to pack into building blocks for houses. Because the grass side faced up, these houses were naturally called "sod houses." There is a Sod House Society of America located in Colby,

Kansas. Because he helped build and lived in a sod house, Everett was presented in 1971 with a lifetime membership certificate as one of the Sons and Daughters of the Soddies.

[6] Everett Lee Hunt, "General Specialists," *Quarterly Journal of Public Speaking*, 2 (July 1916), p. 262.

[7] Letter from Hunt to Windt, October 9, 1982.

[8] Information about Pierre University and Huron College is taken from Garner Horton, ed., *Pioneer College: A History of Pierre University and Huron College 1883-1958*, a special edition of *The Huron College Bulletin* (July 1, 1958), pp. 3-30.

[9] Hunt, "Preface to a History of Huron College," (Preliminary Draft), unpublished manuscript, p. 2).

[10] From "In the Days of My Youth," n.d., n.p. The notebook in which this is found is described as "Being an account of myself as I appeared to others, and of others as they appears to me, published by the typewriter of Everett Lee Hunt in the Art Room of Huron College." The notebook contains Hunt's published and unpublished writings as well as typed copies of newspaper articles and other miscellaneous material from his college days.

[11] *Ibid.*

[12] *The Rubaiyat*, 1912-1913, p. 23.

[13] Letter from Hunt to Windt, June 1, 1979.

[14] *The Rubaiyet*, 1912-1913, p. 23.

[15] Taped interview with Hunt, August 10, 1967, in Swarthmore, Pennsylvania.

[16] Typed copy of the newspaper report in Hunt's "In the Days of My Youth," n.p.

[17] *Ibid.*

[18] *Ibid.*

[19] This account is taken from conversations with Hunt and from an undated note he made years later.

[20] "In the Days of My Youth," n.p.

[21] *Pioneer College*, p. 13.

[22] Donald W. Rasmussen, *A History of Speech Education at Huron College 1883-1943*, unpublished M.A. thesis, University of South Dakota, 1949. I am indebted to this study for the information about all activities related to speech during these early days.

[23] See: Karl Wallace, Ed., *History of Speech Education in America* (New York: Appleton-Century-Crofts, Inc., 1954) and especially the following chapters: Marie Hochmuth and Richard Murphy, "Rhetorical and Elocutionary Training in Nineteenth-Century Colleges," pp. 153-177; Mary Margaret Robb, "The Elocutionary Movement and Its Chief Figures," pp. 178-201; Edyth Renshaw, "Five Private Schools of Speech," pp. 301-325; and Donald K. Smith, "Origin and Development of Departments of Speech," pp. 447-470.

[24] Quoted in Rasmussen, p. 6.

[25] *Ibid.*, pp. 8-9. The Colonial Period included, according to Rassmussen, study of physical culture, voice culture, articulation, inflection, quality of tone, pitch, force, time, volume, brilliance and abandonment in rendering, elementary gesture.

[26] *Ibid.*, pp. 18-22.

[27] *Rubaiyat 1911*, p. 13. The December 23, 1912 issue of the *Huron College Bulletin* was devoted to the debate program and contains additional details about Dr. Hoyt, Everett, and the program that year.

[28] Interview, August 10, 1967.

[29] For a brief biographical sketch of Phillips, see: Raymond G. Smith, "Modern Pioneer in Public Speaking," *Quarterly Journal of Speech*, 35 (February 1949), 47-50.

[30] Quoted in Smith, "Modern Pioneer in Public Speaking," 50.

[31] Hunt, "Teacher's Report," for the school year 1914-1915.

[32] See Rasmussen, p. 18.

[33] *Ibid.*, p. 19.

[34] Hunt, "Academic Public Speaking," *Quarterly Journal of Public Speaking*, 3 (January 1917), pp. 31-32. This article contains more information about what Hunt taught in other courses and how he taught.

[35] *Ibid.*, pp. 34 and 35.

[36] From a tape recording of Hunt's seminar on humanism in rhetoric at Temple University, July 1971. His "Teacher's Report" in 1915 demonstrates his memory was not faculty. He noted that minimum attention was given techniques of speaking and "better supplied by the instructor in criticism of real work than by continuous use of formal texts."

[37] Hunt, "Academic Public Speaking," p. 33.

[38] Harrison Ross Steeves and Frank Humphrey Ristine, Eds., *Representative Essays in Modern Thought* (New York: American Book Company, 1913), p. vii.

[39] Rasmussen, p. 22.

[40] *Ibid.*, pp. 22-23.

[41] Bliss Perry, *And Gladly Teach: Reminiscences* (Boston: Houghton, Mifflin, 1935).

[42] Bliss Perry, "The Amateur Spirit," *The Amateur Spirit* (Boston: Houghton, Mifflin, 1904), p. 4.

[43] *Ibid.*, pp. 32-33.

[44] *Webster's New Collegiate Dictionary.*

[45] James A. Winas, "The Need for Research," *Quarterly Journal of Public Speaking, 1* (April 1915), pp. 20-21.

[46] The Research Committee, "Research in Public Speaking," *Quarterly Journal of Public Speaking, 1* (April 1915), p. 25.

[47] Everett Lee Hunt, "The Scientific Spirit in Public Speaking," *Quarterly Journal of Public Speaking, 1* (July 1915), p. 191.

[48] *Ibid.*, p. 193.

[49] Charles H. Woolbert, "The Organization of Departments of Speech Sciences in Universities," *Quarterly Journal of Public Speaking, 2* (January 1916), pp. 70-71.

[50] Hunt, "General Specialists," p. 258.

[51] *Ibid.*, p. 262.

[52] *Ibid.*, p. 263.

[53] C.H. Wollbert, "A Problem in Pragmatism," *Quarterly Journal of Public Speaking, 2* (July 1916), p. 265.

[54] *Ibid.*, pp. 265-266.

[55] *Ibid.*, pp. 268-271.

[56] *Ibid.*, p. 268.

[57] Hunt, "Academic Public Speaking," p. 27.

[58] *Ibid..*

[59] "C.H.W. to L.E.H. [*sic*]; a rejoinder," p. 36.

[60] *Ibid.*, p. 274.

[61] Carroll C. Arnold, "Rhetoric in America Since 1900," *Re-Establishing the Speech Profession: The First Fify Years*, ed. by Robert T. Oliver and Marvin G. Bauer (No place of publication specified: Speech Association of the Eastern States, September 1959), p. 4.

[62] Hunt, "The Scientific Spirit in Public Speaking," pp. 191-192.

[63] See: Burton J. Bledstein, *The Culture of Professionalism: The Middle Class and the Development of Higher Education in America* (New York: W.W. Norton, 1976).

[64] Walter Lippmann, *A Preface to Morals* (New York: Macmillan, 1929), pp. 9-10.

[65] *Ibid.*, p. 4.

[66] Walter Lippmann, *A Preface to Politics* (New York: Mitchell Kennerley, 1913), p. 4.

[67] Hunt, "An Adventure in Philosophy," *Quarterly Journal of Public Speaking, 3* (October 1917), p. 298.

[68] *Ibid.*, p. 299.

[69] The letter is published in full with opening and closing commentary in *Rhetoric Society Quarterly, 14* (1986), pp. 251-259.

[70] *The Huron Alphomega* (April 10, 1918), p. 1.

3

The Cornell Years

Cornell University is nestled just north of Ithaca and just south of Lake Cayuga in the finger lake country of upper New York state. It was chartered in 1865 as a land-grant college, but ever since Ezra Cornell, the American philanthropist, donated the original endowment of $ 500,000, Cornell has been always a hybrid institution. Morris Bishop noted in 1939 that a college president from the mid-west listed, as distinguished American colleges and as centers of intellectual life, Harvard, Yale, Princeton and "perhaps Cornell." Bishop commented:

> Perhaps Cornell! It has always been the fate of our University to be Perhaps Cornell! A part neither of the aristocratic tradition of the original colonies nor the educational democracy of the great West, half State college, half endowed institution, stoutly liberal and strangely conservative, its activity ranges from research in the noblest mysteries to broadcasting messages on disinfecting brooder houses.[1]

Carl Becker who joined the Cornell history department in 1917 was in a good position to recognize the distinctive atmosphere that permeated Cornell. He had received his Ph.D. from Wisconsin at age 34 (1907), had taught briefly at Pennsylvania State University, Dartmouth, Kansas, and Minnesota. At Cornell, he found an atmosphere that placed more emphasis on people than prescriptions for education and thus created a group of professors who "think otherwise":

> [T]he distinctive quality and flavor of the freedom that flourishes at Cornell . . . includes academic freedom, of course, but it is something more, and at the same time something less, than that—something less formal, something less self-regarding, something more worldly, something, I will venture to say, a bit impudent.[2]

Such a milieu encouraged independent thought and tolerated such colorful faculty as E.B. Titchener and Hendrik Willem van Loon. Indeed, in the case of Titchener, Cornell revered him. Titchener presided over the Psychology Department in which he allowed no kind of psychology except his own to be admitted to the curriculum, and he gave his lectures on Tuesdays and Thursdays at 11 o'clock outfitted always in his Oxford gown. No faculty meetings were ever scheduled to conflict with Titchener's classes since the faculty filed in for the lectures and filled the front row seats.[3]

Across campus Van Loon was a legend, albeit for only a short period. A Harvard Ph.D. and former Associated Press correspondent, he joined the History Department in 1915 and immediately became the most popular teacher in the department. "He was an extraordinarily vivid lecturer," Bishop wrote "illustrating his evocations of the past with rapid sketches on large sheets of brown paper, which he would immediately tear off and trample underfoot."[4] Unfortunately, he seemed better at dramatic lecturing than at getting all his facts right about the European history he was hired to teach. In 1917 he was dismissed, but fortunately for Cornell he was replaced by Becker.

When Everett Hunt came to Ithaca in the fall of 1918, he found a campus in the throes of change. The War was on, and Cornell had become a military school. The War Department had organized the Students' Army Training Corps and contracted with Cornell (and other colleges and universities) to give inductees special academic and military training.[5] The War Department paid tuition, room and board which was a financial god-send to the University. Official figures for 1918 listed 1,696 of these soldiers enrolled on campus along with the regular 848 civilian men, 800 women, and 166 graduates.[6]

This enormous influx of soldier-students had created the need for additional teachers which had been the reason for Winans hiring Hunt. But the Department of Public Speaking was also in the midst of change. Only two years before, Winans had persuaded President Schurman to separate public speaking from the English Department into a department of its own. Now was the time to consolidate the department and prepare for its growth into a graduate department. To this end Hunt joined a faculty that included James Winans and Alexander Drummond with Lane Cooper providing additional help from his classes in the Classics. Winans would preside over the consolidation of the department, and Drummond over its growth. Hunt would give intellectual substance and direction to it. We can better understand the remarkable scholarly influence of this group if we know something about the remarkable men Hunt joined in 1918.

The Cornell Company

Lane Cooper (1875-1959) was a formidable classics scholar, a prolific writer and translator, and an irascible personality. Bishop wrote of him:. "His force of character and his utter devotion to the great literature of the past brought him a long succession of disciples, who in their turn have preached his message from many a professorial pulpit."[7] His force of character was so great that in 1936 a new department of the Comparative Study of Literature was created, "which was really a Department of Lane Cooper, enabling him to do what he pleased, without harassing or being harassed by the Department of English."[8] This eventual Department was most suitable to Cooper who was equally at home with Plato and Aristotle in the classics as with Chaucer, Dante, Milton, or Shakespeare. And his young student "disciples" regularly gathered round him at his special table in the Coffee House in the basement of Barnes Hall where he held court, "as in a French literary cafe."[9]

Lane Cooper was born on February 4, 1875. His father, Jacob Cooper, was Professor of Greek and Philosophy at Rutgers College, and he had an indelible influence on his son. The younger Cooper was educated at Rutgers Prep and received his B.A. from Rutgers College where he took special honors in Mental Philosophy, Moral Philosophy, Metaphysics and Logic. At Commencement, he played a piano concerto and delivered the Rhetorical Honors Oration, "The Crisis in Armenia."[10] After graduation, he studied medicine briefly at Columbia before transferring to Yale where he received his M.A. in English studying under Professor Albert Stanburrough Cook. In *Experiments in Education*, Cooper wrote: "If I have been of value to my pupils, those pupils owe a heavy debt to Mr. Cook."[11] In 1899 he earned a second M.A. in English, this time from Rutgers, and in 1901 he was awarded the Doctor of Philology from the University of Leipzig. After a year's study at the College de France, he came to Cornell in 1902 and began teaching in the English Department.

When the Department of Oratory was part of the English Department, those who sought advanced degrees in this subject usually were supervised by Cooper. Even in the early days after Speech became a separate department, Cooper directed many doctoral dissertation in rhetoric, and included among his students Alexander Drummond (1918), Herbert Wichelns (1922), and Hoyt Hudson (1923). As long as he was active, Cooper attracted graduate students from rhetoric and public address, and few would graduate (or be allowed to graduate) without taking at least one course with him.

By the time of Hunt's arrival Cooper had already established himself as a classical scholar and literary critic. In 1907 he edited a volume entitled *Theories of Style*. By 1918, he had published the following: *A Concordance of the Poems of Williams Wordsworth* (1911); a translation of the *Poetics of Aristotle* (1913); *Aristotle on the Art of Poetry* (1913); *Methods and Aims in the Study of Literature* (1915); *A Concordance to the Works of Horace* (1916); and *The Greek Genius and Its Influence* (1917). And this list does not include the many speeches and articles he published during that time. But for students of rhetoric it would be his translation of the *Rhetoric of Aristotle* that he would gain his fame. Published in 1932 and still in print, Cooper's translation with his notes and introduction remains one of the most popular editions for students in classical rhetoric.

Cooper's life was devoted to scholarship and to Cornell, so much so that he never married and urged others to follow suit. Marriage would only distract one from the pursuit of scholarship and teaching. As Everett told the story, Cooper had a housekeeper and a pet dog for companions for many years. When both died in the same year, an older and wiser Cooper changed his tune and exhorted students to marry so as not to suffer the loneliness of declining years.[12]

Professor Denis Condon noted three themes in Cooper's work that provided a larger mission for his teaching and writing: (1) a true rhetoric must be based on the substance, not the methods of expression; (2) scholarship should be orderly and united with the culture at large; and (3) teaching and scholarship should be at the service of humankind.[13] In *Two Views of Education*, a collection of his essays and papers from his earliest days, he noted, "good rhetoric is the art of the good and successful lover. As such, it is indispensable to the teacher, for he may be defined as the lover of humanity . . . . It is the art which he must strive to acquire who would introduce form and order into the minds of men."[14]

In contradistinction, Cooper castigated the teaching of English in America where it had, according to him, become a sophistical art: "And a sophistical art it will remain so long as the emphasis is laid on expression, and not upon the truth and value of what is to be uttered; nay until the pupils are taught to be silent until it is clear they have something to say."[15] He exhorted others to be orderly learners, organizers of knowledge and to aspire to the essential powers of leadership, "the best scholar, serving his country to the utmost, may be defined as the best men studying the best things in the best way; and whatever else the best may imply, it means first of all a thorough and orderly procedure."[16] It was Cooper's devotion to "studying the best things in the best way" that earned him his reputation both as teacher and scholar. Such standards earned Cooper respect, but did not endear him to his colleagues or students.

Hunt remembered him as a "very vigorous, authoritative" man who believed that his work in the classics, especially his translations and interpretations of Aristotle's *Poetics*, had not been sufficiently appreciated.[17] Hunt respected Cooper, but they were not friends. Among Hunt's papers, I found an off-print of Cooper's essay, "The Climax," published in 1924 by *Sewanee Review*. Hunt had been at Cornell for six years at this time, but the off-print is autographed with the simple words: "With regards of the author."

Nonetheless, Lane Cooper had an informal and influential relation with graduate students in speech and drama at Cornell. They took courses from him. He directed dissertations of some of the most eminent early graduates of Cornell. And his forceful personality as well as his ideas had an influence on all who came in contact with him, some attracted, some repulsed.

One of his students was Alexander Drummond, who was to succeed James Winans as Chairman of the Department of Speech and Drama in 1920 and who later enjoyed a reputation as one of the foremost academic instructors of drama in the twentieth century.

Despite a withered leg, he was a vigorous man:

> He is a big man, in every sense of the word. He can be right almost all of the time without irritating his friends. He drives himself pitilessly and gets things done,—even by under-graduates. He pretends that he doesn't know anything; he can't decide where to eat dinner and he doesn't know till an hour before the boat sails whether he is going to Europe or not. Yet, everyone at Cornell goes to him for advice, and in every organization of which he is a member his opinion is decisive.[18]

Little wonder that he was known as "The Boss" at Cornell.

Alexander Drummond was born in Auburn, New York on July 14, 1884. Like Winans, he was a graduate of Hamilton College. A word needs to be said about Hamilton College at this point. Donald K. Smith noted that perhaps "no college in America has given more ancient and persistent emphasis to speech instruction than has Hamilton College."[19] The Hamilton system of instruction was created by Dr. Henry

Mandeville, who came to the College in 1841 and for eight years worked ceaselessly to give public speaking prominence on campus. He was so successful that by 1902 the Department of Elocution and Rhetoric was listed first among the instructional divisions of the College, and the method of teaching was universally known as the Mandeville system.[20] Both Drummond and Winans were well-immersed in the system by graduation. More important, each had been drilled in the central importance of the subject to the well-rounded and liberally educated student.

Drummond joined the faculty at Cornell in 1907 as an instructor. In 1909 he earned his M.A. degree in English from his alma mater and later in 1918 received his Ph.D. in English Literature from Cornell. His principal interest was drama, and in 1912 took over the Cornell Dramatic Club which Winans had organized in 1909. During the years 1912-1917, in addition to his teaching duties, he coached football at Cascadilla Preparatory School in Ithaca. For a year, 1918-1919, he taught at Cascadilla before returning to Cornell in September, 1919.

In 1920 he was named chairman of the Department of Public Speaking and for the next 20 years presided over the expansion of offerings in rhetoric and public address as well as developing the drama section of the department into a distinguished academic theatre and a doctoral granting program. It was Drummond who encouraged Hunt to offer the 1920 seminar in Classical Rhetoric and taught it with him. And Drummond lent his name as "co-editor" to the first book Everett published so as it get it published.

As a teacher, Drummond could always think "up more questions than any other two people put together."[21] Hudson went on to remark:

> His classroom method is aimed at bringing out a fair interpretation of the thought of others and a clear formulation of one's own. In his discussion of papers read before him, as in all of his associations with a student, this teacher contrives to make a person think and act for himself. His method might be described as controversial and critical. Perhaps Socrates has something to do with it. Students recall no instances of being told precisely what to accept or to believe, or what must be done.[22]

I recite this description of Drummond's teaching for two reasons. Hudson said that many of the students at Cornell did their best work at the initiation of Drummond, regardless of whether they were in public speaking or theatre. Also, Hal Harding who received his doctorate from Cornell once told me that some of his early teachers imitated Drummond's method of teaching just as Harding's contemporaries imitated Wichelns' method later on.

Drummond presided over the growth and development of the Cornell department just as Winans had fought to create it in the first place.

James A. Winans (1872-1956) was one of the giants who led teachers of public speaking out of the elocutionary age and into the modern era of sound instruction and academic respectability. Through his work at Cornell, his central role in the formation of both the Public Speaking Conference of the New England and the North Atlantic States (1910) and the National Association of Academic Teachers of Public Speaking (1915), and finally his vigorous advocacy of the importance of rigorous academic standards for studying and teaching public speaking, Winans holds a special place in the history of the speech profession rivalled only by James O'Neill and perhaps a few others.[23] Herbert Wichelns rightly described him in 1957 as a "fixed star, securely placed in the academic heavens."[24]

Winans was born in 1872 in Sidney Center, New York. He received his B.A. degree (Phi Beta Kappa) from Hamilton College with departmental honors in Greek and Latin, ethics, rhetoric and oratory, psychology and logic. Three years later he received his Master's degree from Hamilton and his LL.B. from Cornell in 1907 though he never actually practiced law. First he taught in high schools, then joined the faculty at Cornell in 1899 as Instructor of Elocution and Oratory, later promoted to full Professor of Public Speaking in 1914. Except for a year at the University of California (1902-1903), he remained the guiding spirit for instruction in public speaking at Cornell until 1920. Like Hunt, he never earned a doctorate.

When he came to Cornell in 1899, he joined a fellow Hamiltonian, Duncan Campbell Lee, who was redirecting the goals and methods for teaching of public speaking, which at that time was only a division within the Department of English. Lee was attempting to change public speaking from elocution to courses "more suited to the use of law students, to the scientific and experimental climate of the Cornell of that day, to the notions of Andrew D. White."[25] According to Waterman Hewett, Lee was attempting to "enlarge the powers of observation, memory, comparison, and reason."[26] Winans joined in this effort with his customary enthusiasm. By 1911 he privately printed *Public Speaking* in which he brought modern psychological findings, William James's concepts in particular, to bear on the principles of speaking. The book was originally for "trial use" at Cornell. Drummond wrote that Winans adapted "Lee's adaptation of [E.N.] Kirby's [author of *Public Speaking and Reading*] ideas, expanded and humanized" them. Four years later, the Century Company published the first edition of what was to become many editions of *Public Speaking*. It became the most influential textbook in public speaking of the twentieth century and set the standard for all others that would follow. James O'Neill wrote of it:

> No other book dealing with the problem of speaking ever presented the results of so much and such accurate study in psychology. With 'attention' as the 'key-word,' Winans has written a book at once sound psychologically, free from the common, external, mechanical approach to specific problems, and at the same time clear, simple, interesting. The book is probably not the last word on the psychology of public speaking. Its author neither claims nor desires it to be. But, it is, it seems to me, the most authoritative word that has ever been spoken on this subject.[27]

Such high praise was richly deserved. Winans had placed public speaking on a sound psychological footing. Equally important, he stressed the need for a conversational quality in presentation, a clear break from the mechanical rules for the delivery of speeches advocated by elocutionists. The commercial publication of *Public Speaking* in 1915 coincided with the establishment of the National Association of Academic Teachers of Public Speaking, and thus became *the* new textbook for a new academic organization, became *the* modern textbook for a modern approach to public speaking.

Nineteen-fifteen was significant in another way for Winans. For some time previously he had been agitating the Dean at Cornell to separate speech from English, but with little success. The "field" of public speaking, the Dean insisted, lacked a "literature" (scholarly publications, that is), apparently a prerequisite for recognition as an independent department. When the first issue of the *Quarterly Journal of Public Speaking* was published, Winans marched into the Dean's office and slapped down a copy of the journal stating: "Now we have a literature."[28] Soon thereafter, he also had a department with himself as Chairman.

By this time Winans was a formidable figure. He had been instrumental in the creation of regional and national professional organizations, he had published the most influential book in the new profession, and he had established a new department at Cornell. Little wonder among his colleagues he was known as "The Chief." But there was another side of him that Drummond caught:

James A. Winans

I never heard of 'the Chief' making a speech except under extreme provocation; and as he is an extremely hard man to provoke, most will never hear him make a speech at all. But those who have had the pleasure of hearing him at his best, before members of his own profession, know with what sly slow-dripping, riotous humor he can sugar the salt of his sad wisdom; with what tonic shrewdness he can interrupt a flow of his own lugubrious folly, and roll up the warm-hearted applause of those who know he is their most watchful critic—and their friend.[29]

But for the five more years he would remain at Cornell he would be both friend and critic as he nurtured his newly created department. And it would be this department during the ten years from 1915-1925 that would develop the Cornell tradition in modern rhetoric, a tradition that would have profound influence on the course of the new profession for the next 50 years.

Hunt's Early Days at Cornell

In the mainstream of academic life, from the broad prairies of South Dakota to the hills and finger lakes of New York, Hunt joined in a new adventure in academe. No longer a college instructor, but now an assistant professor at a university, he had entered professional academic life and now sought to adjust to its requirements. Such adaptation meant significant changes.

The major change was not professional, but personal. His new position and financial equilibrium allowed him to propose to his college sweetheart, Dorothy Rossman. And so he did. She accepted, and they were married on June 24, 1919. She had lived in small South Dakota towns and under near-frontier conditions, out on the family "claim." According to their son, Alan, she "liked to say that if Laura Ingalls Wilder hadn't written 'Little House on The Prairie,' and the other books that followed, she could and would have written them herself."[30] The new Mrs. Hunt brought to Cornell and later to Swarthmore a warm acceptance of people of all sorts for themselves, without some of the traditional eastern concerns about ancestry and wealth. The Hunts' shared love of music and their love for one another sustained them as they sought to adjust to the new circumstances and opportunities in Ithaca.

Having a faculty position at a university meant assuming some of the standards of professionalism, not the least of which was seeking an advanced degree. Hunt was now surrounded by the laboratories and card catalogs Woolbert had described, and he was situated in a university setting that was slowly accepting the German ideal of graduate education. For Hunt advancement at Cornell meant pursuing an advanced degree. After all, he still had only a B.A. in classics from Huron College when he accepted the position at Cornell, even though he was appointed as an assistant professor.

During the summers of 1918 to 1921 Hunt journeyed back to the University of Chicago to take courses in philosophy. With the completion of his thesis, *Dialectic as a Method*, in 1922 he earned his Master's degree in philosophy.

His writing began to change also. He began to contribute reviews of books to the *Quarterly Journal*, among them: Dobson's *The Greek Orators*, Thurber's *Eloquence*, Peterson's biography of Cicero, and many others. Hunt also contributed two essays to the *Quarterly Journal*: "Plato on Rhetoric and Rhetoricians" (June, 1920); and "Dialectic: A Neglected Mode of Argument" (June, 1921). These were quite different from the articles he had penned during his Huron days. They were more in the tradition of scholarly articles than the earlier ones that were essentially polemics. Both essays came from his studies at the University of Chicago. The "Plato" piece was a forerunner of the classic "Plato and Aristotle on Rhetoric and Rhetoricians" that he would complete five years later. The essay on dialectic came directly from his master's thesis. As a result of his work Hunt was elected in 1922 as president of the Eastern Public Speaking Conference. These essays and reviews, his graduate degree from Chicago, and his professional work were Hunt's attempts to adjust to the requirements of a university department and to establish his credentials as a serious scholar.

But at the same time he launched *The [Huron College] Alumni Quarterly*, which he conceived of as a literary magazine as well as a report on alumni activities. In addition to news about the college and its graduates, Hunt, who edited the *Quarterly*, wrote occasional pieces about various educational and cultural subjects, and he solicited poems, essays, and book reviews from others (most notably Hoyt Hudson). Hunt remained as editor of the *Quarterly* for six years from 1919 to 1925 when he left Cornell to go to Swarthmore. The little magazine gave him an outlet for his literary aspirations at a time when he was struggling to establish his scholarly credentials.

The final change in his position at Cornell came when James Winans resigned in 1920 to accept an appointment at Dartmouth. That story has been told many times, but needs to be summarized to understand how it affected Hunt's position at Cornell.

For some time Dartmouth had been trying to lure Winans away from Cornell. He had repeatedly rebuffed their offers. Finally, he decided to make such an outlandish demand of what it would take to move him from Cornell that Dartmouth would quit bothering him. He demanded an $ 8,000 salary and the condition that he would always remain the highest paid faculty member at Dartmouth. Much to his surprise officials at Dartmouth accepted his terms, and he felt that he could not refuse the offer. And so an era at Cornell came to an end.

What is mystifying is why Cornell did not attempt to match the offer from Dartmouth. Did Winans attempt to negotiate with the university where he had spent 20 productive years, or did he believe that he was morally compelled to accept the Dartmouth offer since he himself had set the terms? Equally intriguing is the question of why the "young turks" in the department (Hunt, Wichelns, Caplan and Utterback) as well as Drummond did not press the university to keep Winans? There is no credible evidence that either the university or the department made any significant effort to retain Winans.

Whatever the answers to these questions, the fact remains that Winans left at the end of the school year 1919-1920, that Drummond was named Chairman in November, 1920, and that the department began to expand its offerings and move in different directions once Winans resigned. One of the most important changes was the establishment of a seminar in classical rhetoric beginning in September, 1920.

The 1920 Seminar in Classical Rhetoric

During the Winans years the course offerings in the new department were limited. The Cornell catalogue for these years lists the following: 4 sections of *Public Speaking* in the first term (each taught by a professor) and 2 sections in the second term (each taught by an instructor/graduate student); two terms of *Voice Training* (Assistant Professor Muchmore), two terms of *Oral Reading* (Muchmore); two terms of *Argument and Debate* (Assistant Professor Hunt); two terms of *Advanced Public Speaking* (Professor Winans). One term courses in *Principles of Speech Preparation* (Winans) and *Oral Expression for Architects* (offered in the College of Architecture) were also offered. One general graduate seminar (called "Seminary" in the catalogues) was offered throughout the year that was for "the study of special subjects in the history, literature, psychology, and pedagogy of speech" and conducted by Professor Winans "and other members of the staff."[31]

Five years after Winans left the course offerings had greatly expanded. For the year 1924-1925 the department offered the following courses:

1. *Public Speaking* (8 sections in first term; 5 sections in second term) "Planned to give the fundamentals of speech preparation and to help in the acquisition of a simple, direct manner of speaking. The '86 Memorial Prize for declamation is awarded in connection with this course." Instructors: Professor Drummond, Assistant Professors Muchmore, Hunt, and Wichelns, and Messrs. Hannah, Thomas, Hultzen, and Woehl. [Two other courses in public speaking designated as 1 a. and 1 b. were offered during the year with comparable descriptions and instructors. These apparently were for those who had not done well in the regular courses because the catalogue notes that they "repeat" the work done in Public Speaking 1.]

8. *Voice Training* (Muchmore and Hannah).

10. *Oral Reading* (Muchmore and Hannah).

12. *Argument and Debate* (Hunt and Wichelns). "The application of rules of evidence, types of argument, analysis, detection of fallacies, dialectic method, and parliamentary law to public

debate and discussion. Illustrative material will be drawn from the debates on the adoption of the Federal Constitution and from the Lincoln-Douglas campaigns."

15. *Persuasion and the Forms of Public Address* (Drummond). "Advanced public speaking; problems of interest, persuasion and rhetorical technique; critical reading of typical master-pieces; composition and delivery of various types of public address."

16. *Classical Rhetoric* (Hunt) First term. "Rhetorical theory of Plato, Aristotle, Isocrates, Cicero, and Quintilian."

17. *British Orators* (Muchmore) Second term. "An intensive study of selected British orations and addresses."

18. *History of Rhetoric and Oratory* (Wichelns) First term, but not given in 1924-1925.

19. *American Debate* (Hunt) Second term, but not given in 1924-1925.

20. *Problems and Methods* (Drummond) First term and for graduate credit.

25. *Advanced Course for Teachers* (Muchmore) Second term. "Principles, theories and methods in speech training, phonetics, and correction of defective speech."

30. *Dramatic Interpretation* (Drummond) Both terms. "Theory of dramatic interpretation, training in the direction and production of plays, emphasis on the oral interpretation of dramatic literature."

40. *Seminary* (Drummond) Both terms and "primarily for graduate students." "For the study of special problems in rhetoric, public address, speech training, and dramatic interpretation."

These expanded offerings coincided with the development of the graduate program, but undoubtedly such offerings were sparked in the direction they took by the famous 1920 seminar in classical rhetoric.

Hoyt Hudson, a graduate student in the seminar, noted: "Drummond took over the chairmanship that fall [1920], and, among other things, he wanted to build up the graduate work in rhetoric and public speaking. So he and Everett Hunt founded a seminar."[32] This was the first graduate seminar in classical rhetoric taught in a department of public speaking in the twentieth century, and became a landmark in graduate education as well as a touchstone for publications by the small band of scholars at Cornell. It ran through both terms of the school year.

In actuality, Hunt was the driving force behind the seminar. It was his brainchild. Drummond was listed as teaching it because he was the only one on the faculty with a doctorate. Hunt still had not completed his master's and therefore could not officially offer a graduate course.

More important, the content of the course reflected Hunt's interests. Prior to this time, only general subjects had been offered in this seminar. Of all the possible subjects that could have provided the focus for building up graduate courses in the department, classical rhetoric was chosen. Hunt was working on his graduate degree in philosophy concentrating on Plato, and so an investigation of the classical roots for a modern conception of rhetoric was a natural topic for him. Drummond certainly concurred with this choice due to his work with Lane Cooper. But as Everett later said, he founded the seminar: "In 1920, with the support of A.M. Drummond, head of the dept. I gave the first seminar in classical rhetoric offered in America. Drummond wanted to build up graduate work in rhetoric and public speaking. We studied Plato and the sophists, Aristotle, Cicero, and Quintilian."[33] It was upon this foundation in the classics that the Cornell tradition in rhetoric would be built, and a solid foundation it proved to be. It would provide the core and contours for all subsequent studies in rhetoric at Cornell.

We can be certain that the following people were members of this initial seminar: Hunt, Drummond, Harry Caplan, Herbert Wichelns, and Hoyt H. Hudson.[34] Probably William Emil Utterback, who had followed Hunt to Cornell, was also a member since he was a graduate student at the time although Hunt did not list him later as one of the students.

It might be appropriate at this place to say a few words about these younger members—Caplan, Wichelns, and Hudson—of the seminar. These were the "young turks" of the new post-Winans era, and together with Hunt, they would forge new frontiers in graduate work and research in rhetoric that would dominate the profession for the next 45 years. About this group Hunt observed: "They were conscious of being pioneers but preferred to be pioneers with a tradition."[35]

In his tribute to Harry Caplan upon his retirement Hunt wrote: "You had a better training in the study of classics than any of our group, and were a guiding spirit in the development of our seminar in classical rhetoric."[36] Certainly this homage to Caplan was not an understatement.

Harry Caplan was born in Hoag's Corners, New York on January 7, 1896. He graduated from Albany High School as both the prize winner in Greek and valedictorian. He earned his B.A. degree from Cornell in 1916 (Phi Beta Kappa) and completed his M.A. in 1917. He spent one year on fellowship and another in the army before returning to Cornell to pursue his doctorate in Classics. His association with Cooper certainly was one reason for his involvement in the Department of Public Speaking. Another personal reason was that he was Jewish. Anti-semitism was a fact at Cornell. Although he glosses over it a bit, Bishop noted that it existed:

> Anti-Semitism, barely perceptible in the early days, became more pronounced, as a mass movement from Polish ghettoes and the Ukraine disturbed the social structure of our cities. The fraternities ceased, generally, to enroll Jewish members, and Jewish fraternities appeared. The first was Zeta Beta Tau, in 1907. Jewish students complained of discrimination on the publications and in other activities. They were probably justified; but of course, one never knows when one is discriminated against as a group member and when as an individual.[37]

Harry Caplan knew.

As he neared the end of his first year of doctoral studies, he received a letter from his faculty adviser in Classics (but signed by other members of the faculty as well) suggesting that he would be better able to find a teaching position in a high school than a college or university because he was a Jew. The fact of the matter was, they averred, Jews were generally barred from teaching positions in higher education.[38] Caplan anguished over the advice from his professors, as a series of letters he exchanged with his brother demonstrates, and even thought of following his brother's advice to get a law degree and join the family law firm.[39] It is unclear how he made the move from the Classics department to Public Speaking. But the next year (1918) he joined the Public Speaking Department as an instructor, and thus participated in the 1920 seminar.

Later, of course, Harry Caplan transferred to the Classics Department (1924), became Chairman (1930), and was appointed Goldwin Smith Professor of the Classical Languages and Literature (1940). During his distinguished career as translator and historian of classical and medieval rhetoric, he translated the Loeb Classical Library's version of *Rhetorica ad Herennium* and contributed mightily to the study of the history of rhetoric. Helen North rightly said of Caplan that he was the "acknowledged master of the historical study of ancient and medieval rhetoric in his generation, the father of that discipline in our own country."[40]

Herbert Wichelns had more influence on rhetorical criticism than any other academic scholar of the twentieth century, even as he probably published less

Herbert A. Wichelns

than another other major scholar. Beginning with his legendary essay, "The Literary Criticism of Oratory" (1925) to his direction of Edwin Black's doctoral dissertation which was turned into another landmark book, *Rhetorical Criticism: A Study in Method* (1965), he exerted either a direct and indirect influence on practically every critic of rhetorical discourse not only at Cornell but throughout the country.

Herbert A. Wichelns was born on December 29, 1894 in Brooklyn, New York. He earned his B.A. from Cornell in 1916 and became an instructor in public speaking the following year as he began his graduate studies under Lane Cooper. After a brief stint in the army during the War, he returned to Cornell to complete his graduate education. He assisted Hunt in teaching public speaking and was a member of the 1920 seminar. Wichelns was awarded his doctorate in 1922. He taught briefly at Dartmouth, New York University and the University of Pittsburgh, from which he was asked to leave because he persisted in smoking on campus in violation of the strict rules against smoking.[41]

He then returned to Cornell in 1924.

Wichelns had a long and distinguished career at Cornell. He served as president of the Eastern Public Speaking Conference (1930), as first editor of *Communication Monographs* (1930-1932) though no issues were published during his tenure, and as president of the Speech Communication Association of America (1937). From 1926 until his retirement in 1962, he directed the work of the "second and third generations" of Cornellians (including Donald Bryant, Karl Wallace, Harold Harding, Wilbur Samuel Howell, Leland Griffin and Edwin Black among others) who spread the Cornell tradition far and wide among academic departments of speech. More than any other Cornellian, he not only contributed to the original ideas of the little Cornell group, he translated them into a sustaining tradition.

Finally, there was Hoyt Hudson, pre-eminent Renaissance man in a group of Renaissance men. Among these original Cornellians there seems little dispute that Hudson was the most original, most brilliant, and most prolific of them all.

Hudson was born in Norfolk, Nebraska on July 6, 1893. He met Everett Hunt in South Dakota where

they both graduated from Huron College. After graduation Hudson spent the next several years teaching in high schools, working in lumberyards, and writing poetry and criticism. He earned an M.A. degree from the University of Denver in 1913. When Winans went to Dartmouth, Hunt invited Hudson to Cornell just in time to join the 1920 seminar. During his graduate student days, he published two of the most important early essays to come out of Cornell: "The Field of Rhetoric," (1923) and "Rhetoric and Poetry" (1924). He taught briefly at Swarthmore and the University of Pittsburgh before settling into his position as Professor of Rhetoric and Oratory and Chairman of the Department of English at Princeton (1927-1942). His last three years were spent at Stanford University until his untimely death on June 13, 1944.

At his death Hudson's books included: *Poetry of the English Renaissance* (edited with J.W. Hebel); *A First Course in Public Speaking* (with James Winans); *Principles of Argument and Debate* (with J.W. Reeves); an edition of John Hoskins's *Directions for Speech and Style*; and translations of Kant's *Religion Within the Limits of Reason Alone* (with T.M. Greene), Erasmus's *The Praise of Folly*, and Thomas Moffet's *Nobilis* (with Virgil Hetzel). His posthu-

Hoyt Hudson

mously published books included: *The Epigram in the English Renaissance*, *Educating Liberally*, and *Celebration* (a collection of some of Hudson's own poems.). Everett Hunt often said that he was "some kind of genius," and rarely spoke of Hudson without a mixture of love and awe in his voice.

These were the men of the seminar who together with Alexander Drummond would examine the ancient roots for their new profession and would attempt to replant those roots in modern soil.

For a year this small band embarked upon "voyages of discovery through Plato's *Phaedrus* and *Gorgias*, Aristotle's *Rhetoric*, Cicero's *De Oratore*, and Quintilian's *Institutiones*."[42] In addition, they picked up something along the way about Isocrates and the sophists. Each of the members was thoroughly conversant with Greek. Caplan, of course, was a classics major. Wichelns had won a Greek prize in high school. Hunt and Hudson had read Greek with a clergyman instructor at Huron College. Drummond's role, as it usually was his preference, was to ask questions to help clarify thinking or point people in new directions:

Alexander Drummond

> There was Drummond, you see, asking questions, never knowing anything but showing an almost pathetic willingness to learn. He wasn't exactly dull, but he was stubborn as all get out. Somehow we couldn't let him down; we had to educate him. It is true that he seemed to have read everything . . . . When we had been especially adventurous and had marched out on a lone hunt, whether in our reading or our thinking, we were likely to meet Drummond there—coming back.[43]

Drummond seemed to serve as the classroom catalyst.

No one has commented directly in writing about Hunt's contribution, but it must have been considerable. He planned the seminar and in his own quiet way conducted it. As Wichelns commented in another context, there was Everett: "[a] mind detached, reflective, unhurried, endlessly ingenious in perception and combination . . . "[44] He chose the readings and made the assignments. Judging from his later long work on Plato, Aristotle and the sophists, which covers much of the ground that was explored in the seminar, one can imagine the significant role he played.

Most important was the fact that this small band became excited about applying classical principles to a modern study of rhetoric and public speaking. They were not content to be philologists of classical rhetoric, but sought, as Donald C. Bryant noted, to find the "relation of rhetoric to the modern world and for a definition of [the] function" of rhetoric in the twentieth century.[45] With such a wide net cast, little wonder that Hudson wrote of the seminar: "Things began to happen. We found that there were articles we wanted to write. We saw chances to apply classical dogmata in our dealings with modern material. We suddenly discovered that swatting over old books or swinking over long papers was fun."[46]

And write they did. Between the years 1920 to 1925, the group was prolific in their contributions to the *Quarterly Journal*.

Hunt: "Plato on Rhetoric and Rhetoricians," (June 1920); "Dialectic: A Neglected Method of Argument," (June 1921); "Adding Substance to Form in Public Speaking Courses," (June 1922); "Knowledge and Skill," (February 1923); "The Teaching of Public Speaking in Schools of Theology," (November 1924).
Hudson: "Can We Modernize the Study of Invention?" (November 1921); "The Field of Rhetoric," (April 1923); "Rhetoric and Poetry," (April 1924).
Wichelns: "Research," (June 1923); "Our Hidden Aims," (November 1923); "Analysis and Synthesis in Argumentation," (June 1925).
Caplan: "The Latin Panegyrics of the Empire," (February 1924).
Drummond: "Graduate Work in Public Speaking," (April 1923).

One might add to these, the contributions of other Cornellians during this time: William Utterback's two articles on the psychology of argumentation (1924 and 1925); Wayland Parrish's piece on style in extemporaneous speaking (1924); Raymond Howes's comparison of American and English debating (1925); Robert Hannah's study of Burke's audience (1925); Marvin Bauer's "The Influence of Lincoln's Audience on His Speeches" (1925). No other school—be it college or university—could match this explosion of research and writing. Some of these writings became classics. And this outburst culminated in the volume of original studies presented to James Winans in 1925, *Studies in Rhetoric and Public Speaking in Honor of James A. Winans* by his pupils and colleagues, which contained two of the most influential pieces written in the modern era: Hunt's "Plato and Aristotle on Rhetoric and Rhetoricians," and Wichelns's "The Literary Criticism of Oratory." All in all, it was a staggering feat by this small band of novice scholars who had only their own rediscovery of the ancients and their own good sense to guide them. From these would come a multitude of additional studies, not only by the original Cornellians but by the second and third generation that would follow and by fledgling scholars at other schools who would try to meet the high standards set before them.

The spark for all this activity was the 1920 seminar. It is ironic that Everett Hunt, who had decried specialized scholarship, presided over a seminar that generated the first flowering of such scholarship. It is doubly ironic that Everett Hunt, who planned the seminar, did not offer it again. In fact, it appears that he did not offer another graduate course until after his retirement when he became a visiting professor at various universities. He could not offer the 1920 seminar under his sole direction because he had only a B.A. degree. Afterwards, he was prohibited from teaching graduate courses even after he received his master's and concentrated instead on upper division courses for juniors and seniors, one or two of which presumably could be taken for graduate credit. Swarthmore, his next and final stop in his career, was an undergraduate college. Hunt's primary influence on Cornell students was as an undergraduate teacher. Wichelns once wrote of him: "the originality and subtlety of his insights did not lend themselves to systematic formulation, the students he inspired took their advanced degrees under others [principally Wichelns] but his example of the true scholarly mind, inquiring, noting, combining, has put the present generation of graduate students, and their teachers, heavily in his debt."[47] It may be appropriate at this time to consider Everett Hunt as a teacher.

Everett Hunt on Teaching

In 1918 Everett published a essay entitled "Creative Teaching in Wartime." World War I had created a new situation on college campuses, already described in this chapter, and brought a new kind of student to higher learning. The Student Army Training Corps, Everett noted, brought young men to colleges to prepare them to fight the war, and thus changed the function and purpose of college teaching: "Teachers of liberal arts face many perplexities in adapting themselves to the military regime .... They know that for the time their own aims and purposes are secondary; that their students must be more concerned with defeating Kultur than with receiving culture."[48] Within these temporary conditions imposed by war, Hunt stated that the need to be creative was even more important that ever. These students would be at a college only a couple of months, or at most a year. One would indeed have to be creative to teach anything of value in such a short period of time.

But Everett meant more by "creative" than a new kind of teacher who would adapt and respond to the emergency and the peculiar circumstances of the war. For him creative teaching at any time meant enthusiastic teachers who excited new interests among students, who were inspirational, who taught by suggestive glimpses rather than pedantic thoroughness, and who loved their subjects.

Hunt did not believe in teaching techniques of speaking or any other methods of "how to do it." How could one *love* skills or drills? Teaching such things bored him, and he was equally certain such subject matter would bore his students as well. As he said in his remarks at the Temple Conference, he taught ideas —the subjects of student speeches—and paid little attention to the techniques of speaking. Instead, he required his students to do extensive reading, and he asked questions and made suggestions to spark further curiosity and thinking. Hunt saw himself as a guide, a prompter. He expected his students to bring ideas to class, and then he would prod them to pursue those they found of interest, to develop and expand upon them. Hunt aided in this process by suggesting other readings or pointing to overlooked implications.

This neglected essay on teaching is one that beginning teachers might still read with profit. It is the advice of one of our eminent teachers writing enthusiastically about teaching when he was young. It is not a set of precepts or a prescription for teaching, but a lyrical ode to the qualities that he believed made for inspired teaching. The concluding paragraph summarized this lyricism, "Nothing human is foreign to the creative teacher, his own thought is thought-provoking and suggestive of farther reaches, he is filled with the spirit of all life and knows its joys and sorrows, he abides the time when his students shall be moved by the same spirit, and the motive back of all his work is the love of it."[49]

Such were the thoughts of the 28 year old Hunt in his first year of teaching at Cornell.

But how did he put these ideas into practice? Wilbur Samuel Howell, who was an undergraduate in Hunt's course on Argumentation at Cornell, remembered his teaching in those days:

> Although Everett was nominally the Cornell Debate coach, he did not stress college debating in his course in Argumentation. He thought rather of debating as a central enterprise in the political life of a democratic society; the debates in the British parliament, in the Colonial Legislatures of our own country over the ratification or rejection of our Constitution when it was submitted for consideration, the later Lincoln-Douglas debates over the extension of slavery into the Territories—these were what Everett wanted his students to absorb, understand, and use as models in their own development. Everett assigned Foster [author of *Argumentation and Debate*] as an argumentation textbook, but he never taught from its pages. He believed instead in having his students familiarize themselves with the debates of history.
>
> For instance, he had his students read, among other things, the debates over the new Constitution in the colonial legislature of New York. He assigned individual debaters to each one of us, had us master their arguments, asked us to reproduce their arguments in our speeches in class, to stand cross examination upon them, and to answer the objections that their arguments drew from their opponents. The Platonic dialogues, a special feature of Everett's own scholarship, gave us the models to be followed in our own response to cross examination. From this background we learned lessons that turned our student arguments outside of class into Socratic exercises. By those means he made his course in Argumentation teach us history, philosophy, and a lot that we would not have gathered from Foster, although Foster had written a good book on debating.[50]

Raymond F. Howes confirmed this description of Hunt's teaching. He noted that Everett took them through "the Greek Sophists, Roman orators, and the rhetorical treatises of Plato and Aristotle; Edmund Burke and other British orators, the debates over the American Constitution, and the Lincoln-Douglas debates over slavery and national unity." He remembered writing a paper on the sophist, Lysias, and "struggling through the *Federalist* papers; and impersonating Lincoln when we recreated a portion of one of the debates." The textbook was treated "almost as an aside."[51]

However, for his discussions of the Greek rhetoricians and sophists, Hunt put together a notebook of reprints of articles from the *Quarterly Journal* that he called "Studies in Rhetoric." He probably began compiling this collection in 1923 since the latest article in original table of contents was Hudson's "The Field of Rhetoric." Other reprints included: Hudson's "Can We Modernize the Theory of Invention?" Russell Wagner's "The Rhetorical Theory of Isocrates," Paul Shorey's "What Teachers of Speech May Learn from the Theory and Practice of the Greeks," L.G. Rousseau's "The Rhetorical Principles of Cicero and Adams," Hunt's own "Dialectic: A Neglected Method of Argument" and "Plato on Rhetoric and Rhetoricians," as well as Bromley Smith's series of articles on Corax, Gorgias, Prodicus, and Protagoras.[52]

The notebook also contains Hunt's teaching notes, how complete these are one cannot determine, nor can one determine when they were used.[53] They are brief but cover such topics as "Rhetoric & Ethics" (one side of a 5 x 8 inch page) and "Rhetoric & Poetry" (three sides of 5 x 8 inch pages). Another small page lists the following in short order: "Rhetoric & Education," "Rhetoric & Speech," "Rhetoric & Dialectic," "Rhetoric & Propaganda," and "Rhetoric & History." A few remarks follow each. For example, after "Rhetoric & History" Hunt observed: "Rhetorical historians once accepted speeches at their face value in explaining historical events. Uncritical rhetoricians still do. 'Scientific' historians tend to throw out speeches . . . altogether. Speeches should be studied by rhetoricians as representing an influential public justification of policies by rationalization." (Given the additions to the original notebook, Hunt probably used this notebook to teach from at the beginning of his tenure at Swarthmore College.)

Such heady material must have been heady and exciting stuff for undergraduates. C. Harold King, also an undergraduate at this time, recalled:

> No one quite knew how [Hunt] did it. There he would sit, firing everybody's insides from behind that bland exterior. Can you imagine a group of undergraduates touring bookstores on a Saturday afternoon, and then spending Saturday night reading to one another? There must be something queer about a man who could so reverse the course of nature.[54]

Howes concluded that each student "had the feeling that Everett had a direct interest in him as a person."[55] And his 1921 class in Argumentation presented him with a silver vase with the inscription: "To Everett Lee Hunt, Friend and Teacher in happy remembrance of many valued hours spent together in Cornell University." Twenty-one students' names were engraved on the vase.

His "direct interest" extended beyond the classroom.

Some 65 years later, Sam Howell still remembers that at the end of the course in argumentation Hunt invited the class to his home on Cayuga Heights where his wife, Dorothy, served strawberry shortcake under thick whipped cream and invited students to conduct themselves as they wished.[56] Howes recalled Everett getting graduating students jobs, including himself: "On Commencement Day . . . I heard someone calling my name. It was Everett. When I hailed him, he handed me a telegram offering me an appointment as an instructor at the University of Pittsburgh at the then munificent salary of $ 1600 a year."[57] And this "direct interest" did not end with graduation or getting students jobs, but continued throughout a lifetime and was kept going through correspondence, visits, recommendations, above all, a persistent personal concern for the full well-being of each that he thought of as a friend.

But Hunt's method of teaching did not pass without criticism. Part of that criticism came from his original Chairman, James Winans, and another part from members of the profession. When teaching public speaking, he was supposed to be teaching from Winans' *Public Speaking*. However, as with his course in Argumentation, he paid little attention in class to the text. (His copy of *Public Speaking* shows very few of the underlinings or notes in the margins that he liberally sprinkled throughout his other books.) Winans found out about this neglect:

But after two or three years there, he [Winans] came around and said: "I've sat outside the door of your classroom just to hear what was going on and I couldn't see that you've paid any attention to my textbook at all. Now, that textbook is what you're supposed to be teaching and why don't you teach it?"

And I said: "I'd try to do better on that. I'll try to do it."

Well, about that time Dartmouth College offered Winans twice the salary to come to Dartmouth and he left. So, there was no one to compel me to teach Winans' textbook.[58]

Hunt repeatedly said that he and the other Cornellians were proud of the work of Winans, his textbook, and his contributions to the theory of the psychology of public speaking. But that is not what Hunt wanted to teach, nor was that what Hunt believed the central concerns of teaching public speaking ought to be.

Before he left Cornell he would edit a textbook that he could teach from. He called it *Persistent Questions in Public Discussion.* Although the title page lists Drummond as co-editor (indeed his name comes before Hunt's), Drummond had nothing to do with the preparation or editing of the book. His sole contribution was to lend his name so that Everett could get a publisher. The Century Company that published *Persistent Questions* had a Cornell connection. It had published the first commercial edition of Winans' *Public Speaking* (1915) and kept it and subsequent versions (*A First Course in Public Speaking* by Winans and Hudson, 1931, and then *Speech-Making* by Winans and C.K. Thomas, 1938) in print during the years. The continuing success of that volume undoubtedly inclined Century to consider other volumes by people at Cornell. And it was to the Century that the Cornellians would go to get their tribute to James Winans, *Studies In Rhetoric and Public Speaking,* published in 1925, that Drummond would go to for the Speech Association's *A Course of Study in Speech Training and Public Speaking for Secondary Schools; Being the Report of a Special Committee of the National Association of Teachers of Speech* (1925), and Hudson for his *Poetry of the English Renaissance: 1509-1660* (1929), and Drummond once again for his *Problems and Opinions* (1931) as well as Lane Cooper for his translation of Aristotle's *Rhetoric* (1932).

But in 1924 Hunt was not an eminent "name," and Drummond was. Everett was everlastingly grateful for the generosity of Drummond in lending his name so that the book could be published, but he was equally clear that he alone prepared and edited *Persistent Questions,* and that he wrote the introductory pieces of the book.

Persistent Questions in Public Discussion was a different kind of textbook from *Public Speaking* or the other texts that were appearing by members of the Association. It contained no discussion of techniques for speaking. It was a content book. John Dolman, Jr. of the University of Pennsylvania noted that prior to its publication no such anthology had been produced for courses in public speaking although colleagues in English composition had many such books. He observed, "But here is a book of the same kind [as those in English] edited by teachers of public speaking and prepared especially for their own classes—not a book of model speeches for study as such, but a book of stimulating source material, selected with reference to its actual helpfulness in arousing discussion. Those who know the work of Mr. Drummond and Mr. Hunt in other connections need not be told that the book is well done."[59]

Indeed, it was different. It was different from James O'Neill's *Classified Models of Speech Composition* which collected speeches for the purpose of providing models for speaking on "all sorts of occasions," these occasions being the different ways in which speeches were classified and the reason for their selection.[60]

Hunt's book was for thinking: "The purpose of this collection is to provide stimulating material dealing with questions that are constantly before the public." And he wrote: "Selections have been sought which, whatever their date, will provoke further thought concerning fundamental issues on which an educated citizen should have enlightened opinions, and which he should be able to discuss intelligently."[61] He chose two or three essays or speeches to illustrate these persistent public questions. Topics of the volume included: American Character and Ideals, Democracy, Liberty of Thought and Discussion, Economic Society, Education, Religion, Racial Problems (which included an address by W.E.B. DuBois), War and Peace, International Relations, Public Duty and Public Discussion. In "A Word To Teachers" he wrote that he had "sought stimulating and provocative readings which adequately state conflicting views on a series of selected public questions" and that these selections were intended "to arouse interest in further investigation and discussion of ideas which are central in our political and social thinking."[62] The Appendices presented teachers with questions for discussions on each of the readings, suggestions for further readings on each chapter, and some additional topics for the discussion of each issue.

Everett repeatedly said that *Persistent Questions in Public Discussion* best represented what he truly wanted for the profession and what he most wanted to do with his teaching and writing. He would often chuckle with amusement that his prominence rested on "Plato and Aristotle on Rhetoric and Rhetoricians" and that he was thought of by younger generations as a classicist. On one occasion, he even went so far as to say that he had written "Plato and Aristotle" for the purpose of establishing his scholarly credentials so that no one could attack him for being an amateurish dilettante when he spoke out on more significant issues. Such a notion, even if it did come from Everett, is far-fetched, and I took that to be a momentary lapse in his usual well-balanced sense of himself.

Nonetheless, *Persistent Questions* did represent the marriage of form and content that Hunt believed should be the center of rhetorical studies, with a heavy emphasis on substance over technique. He limited the topics to persistent public issues because, as he wrote in one of his Huron essays, he wanted to produce students who will be "leaders of men, who will have an active share in all public affairs."[63] The book was widely used by the next generation of Cornellians as they issued forth to teach in various colleges. It was a severe challenge to teachers who had previously been no more than elocutionists.

Part of the spark for producing *Persistent Questions in Public Discussion* was Hunt's dissatisfaction with having to teach Winans' *Public Speaking* or any other text that dealt solely with methods for speaking or arguing. But what began and may be passed off as a minor disagreement between two faculty members at Cornell later expanded into a major controversy within the new profession. In the June 1922 issue of the *Quarterly Journal* Hunt published an article, "Adding Substance to Form in Public Speaking," that spelled out his approach to what ought to be taught in public speaking courses. The response was immediate and resulted in a panel at the joint convention of the Eastern Public Speaking Conference and the National Association in December, 1922.

The Form Versus Content Controversy

The 1923 meeting of the Eastern Conference of Public Speaking was held at Christmas, 1922 in conjunction with the National Association. The conference had been organized in 1910 by Winans, Wilbur Jones Kay, and Paul M. Pearson, father of Drew Pearson and a dynamic professor at Swarthmore College. The Eastern Conference was the oldest continuing professional organization for teachers of public speaking, the most active regional association, and counted among its members some of the most prominent teachers in New England and the Atlantic states.

The Christmas meeting highlighted the "form versus content" controversy which was in reality a continuation of the previous Woolbert-Hunt debate only along different lines. And it spawned a whole series of articles with other scholars taking up one side or the other.[64]

The point of contention specifically concerned how much attention a teacher should pay to the substance of students' speeches. Should teachers limit their instruction solely to the form or techniques of speaking? Hunt sparked the controversy when he wrote in "Adding Substance to Form in Public Speaking Courses" in 1922 that teachers should pay more attention to *what* students say than to *how* they say it. He argued that the content of a course in public speaking should "include as source material a group of essays or addresses which treat a limited number of fundamental subjects upon which any liberally educated man should be able to speak intelligently and effectively in public."[65] He stated that ideas within the realm of probability, controversial public issues of enduring interest, should provide topics for students' speeches. He excluded informative or other forms of speeches from his courses.

Teachers from the Midwest, especially James M. O'Neill, were once again incensed by Hunt's ideas. Marshalling all his authority as first president of the National Association and first editor of the *Quarterly Journal*, O'Neill came to the joint meeting prepared to exorcise Hunt's heresy.

In his speech to the convention O'Neill charged that "Adding Substance to Form" and William P. Sandford's article, "The Problem of Speech Content," made "the most thorough-going attack upon the worth and dignity of instruction in public speaking that has appeared in our generation."[66] He predicted that if Hunt's and Sandford's ideas were ever adopted by teachers of speech that "courses known as courses in public speaking should, and will, soon disappear from our colleges and universities."[67]

O'Neill accused Hunt of undermining the dignity of teaching the mechanics of speaking, the primary duty of a teacher of speech. He said that the subjects students chose for speeches concern teachers or critics only incidentally:

> Ideas, facts, information, therefore, about tariff, diplomacy, and poverty, and the great principles of liberty, religion, and progress, are legitimately given attention in public speaking only incidentally, only insofar as giving them attention promotes the real purposes of such courses— knowledge of, and proficiency in, public speaking.[68]

O'Neill defined teaching public speaking as teaching techniques of speaking. It was as simple as that. Teachers had no right to venture into the areas of politics, sociology, economics, or ethics, except for academic or professional ethics of, say, plagiarism. Teachers should not prescribe topics for students. They should not provide reading materials for students. O'Neill objected to Hunt's limiting students to speeches on controversial public problems and accused him of being an undemocratic dilettante.

At the same meeting Hunt replied that knowledge is more important that skill. Public speaking, he said, is a liberal art, and the liberal college is a "standing protest against the subordination of life to routine."[69] Teaching only form or skills involved routine and resulted in drudgery. In addition, these skills seldom influence important decisions in life. We should do better, Hunt said, if we were to cultivate a philosophic attitude toward problems and a system of values by which to judge what we ought to do rather than concentrating on acquiring proficiency in the mechanics of speaking:

> If we are free men we do not cast our votes as a result of a particular skill; most of us ought not to choose our profession because of skill; we do not marry through skill, or accept or reject religions through skill, or become conservative or radical, or appreciate nature or select our friends or love our country or hate lying, through skill. For the direction of these choices there is needed all the knowledge that can be obtained in the four short years of its unhampered pursuit.[70]

Instead of drilling students in routine techniques, Hunt would encourage them to explore controversial ideas for the purpose of deciding what values they believe most important. As particular speeches or essays were studied, the specific techniques used by the advocate could be discussed, but that was about the only context in which Hunt was interested in studying them. He reasserted his persistent thesis that methods could not be separated from ideas.

The charge that he was undemocratic involved greater difficulties, especially for this democratic socialist. Hunt replied that restricting students to public issues as subjects for speeches reflected the tradition of the liberal arts, not a political tradition. The liberal arts college, he noted, is exclusive, not inclusive. Some ideas are more important than others. Thus, there is a college of liberal arts, a college of engineering, a medical school, and school of education. In professional schools, skills may be extremely important, but in a liberal arts curriculum, the exploration of ideas is the most important intellectual mission of both teachers and students.[71] Courses in public speaking should strive to be liberal by limiting the topics for student speeches to public issues and the purpose to persuasive speaking.

Wichelns summarized the debate and its effects on members attending the convention:

> Involved was the speech teacher's interpretation of the range of his responsibility. O'Neill would take the student as he was and develop his ability to communicate his present thought by giving

him better technical command of the resources of expression. Hunt wished to stimulate thinking, give wider perspective and deeper insight; in consequence he put less stress on technical improvement. O'Neill was concerned to find a clearly delimited departmental field. Hunt, who had come to the east from the open prairie, naturally said: "Don't fence me in." It was a great battle, in which the attacker's [O'Neill's] hard debating style was well contrasted with his opponent's [Hunt's] more thoughtful reflective approach. It left the members of the Eastern [Public Speaking Conference] unmoved in the end.[72]

But more was at stake than the range of teachers' responsibilities.

Hunt contended that the examination of public issues and the persuasive arguments used to justify them formed the essence of a liberal education and that teaching only skills diverted teachers from their primary responsibility: the education of the liberal person. The controversy no longer involved the academic topic of specialization but now overflowed to the aims of a liberal education. Hunt was asking explicitly whether public speaking can claim to be a liberal art when its teachers eschewed ideas? O'Neill said yes. Hunt said no and provided an alternative perspective to the curriculum of skills and mechanics advocated by O'Neill and his supporters.

But it went beyond even these topics. It was a battle between East and Midwest, between two different conceptions of the field of public speaking. On the one side were O'Neill, Woolbert and the other Midwesterners (as well as some sympathizers in the East.) On the other side were Hunt, Hudson, Wichelns and the other Cornellians as well as W.P. Sanford (and one presumes some kindred spirits in Wisconsin and Illinois). Hoyt Hudson would eventually emerge as chief spokesman for the Cornell group with his essays, "Rhetoric and Poetry" and "The Field of Rhetoric," but the beginnings of this dispute once again originated with Everett Hunt.

Five issues distinguished the two groups from one another.

First, the Midwesterners insisted that speech—oral as opposed to written language—was the defining feature of the new profession.

Second, the Midwesterners sought to develop a curriculum that would draw together all subjects that relied primarily upon spoken language from public speaking to drama to speech correction and oral interpretation.

Third, they sought to make the study of speech a specialized study that would produce specialized research for the new discipline.

Fourth, they insisted that the proper subject-matter for teaching and research was the techniques of how oral language is used and how it can be improved; ideas about public issues interested them only incidentally.

Fifth, the Midwesterners sought to establish a professional academic discipline that would train undergraduates to become proficient in speaking and that would prepare graduate students to become experts in research on speaking.

The Cornellians, led by Hunt and Hudson, came in direct conflict on each of these.

First, the Cornellians insisted that rhetoric was the defining feature of the new profession. Hudson said it well: "Rhetoric does not include all the work done by our present departments of public speaking: it does not include the oral interpretation of literature, nor dramatics, nor studies designed to improve the pronunciation and diction of ordinary conversation."[73] Instead, a field grounded in rhetoric would be centered on persuasion, be it spoken or written.

Second, the Cornellians wanted a curriculum that would be broadly liberal and draw together studies of all subjects that depended on persuasion. Drummond listed these subjects in his article, "Some Subjects for Graduate Study—Department of Public Speaking, Cornell University," in the February, 1923 issue of the *Quarterly Journal*. Among the 129 subjects he listed were: "Rhetoric and Logic," "Rhetoric and Dialectic," "Rhetoric and Probability," "History of the feud between philosophy and rhetoric," "Historical study of rhetoric of declamation as opposed to rhetoric of content," translations of significant rhetorical texts, and so on and on. This article taken with Drummond's other article, "Graduate Work in Public

Speaking," provides the most specific description of the intellectual concerns of the Cornell school of rhetoric as well as the topics that succeeding generations of graduate students at Cornell would investigate.[74]

Third, they believed the study of rhetoric ought to be liberal and humane, not scientific or specialized. Hunt was especially adamant on this point from his first published essay at Huron to his last public statement a year before his death. He believed that making the study of rhetoric or public speaking specialized or scientific or professional would make it into a modern scholasticism cut off from the life-blood of politics and ethics. Instead, he insisted that public speaking could only be liberal and humane if teachers and scholars concentrated their attention on ideas in the realm of probability and examined the various persuasive arguments that prominent figures had used to address those public issues, those "persistent questions in public discussion." It should be remarked that none of the other Cornellians was as adamant about these limitations as Hunt was.

Fourth, they gave the techniques of speaking only a small place in their curriculum of study, and instead they sought to ally the study of rhetoric with the liberal arts, with ethics and politics, with history and literature. The perspective came from classical writers on rhetoric, not from modern social sciences, from an understanding of the history of the subject, not from laboratory experiments. They would broaden their concerns to editorial writers, pamphleteers, advertisers, preachers, lawyers, propagandists, and all sorts of others who depended upon persuasion. Writing later, Loren Reid noted that the Cornell tradition was "more concerned with rhetorical theory than with the criticism of speakers . . . . Its standards are classical, applied venturesomely and imaginatively; it is deeply rooted in literature . . . .[75] In addition, this small group sought to identify the place of rhetoric in the modern world and, as Donald C. Bryant pointed out, its function in intellectual and public affairs.[76]

Finally, the Cornellians sought to establish the intellectual bases for research and the teaching of rhetoric in colleges and universities. They were more concerned that their students be liberally and humanely educated than be professionally trained as specialists as the Midwesterners would train them. Hunt, in particular, believed that if this intellectual base were established and connected with the ancient Greek and Roman conceptions of rhetoric as the center of liberal arts and as the most appropriate preparation for public life (be it in public affairs or education), then professional recognition would follow.

It was on this final issue that Hunt greatly miscalculated. The result of Hunt's ideas would have been that all other departments within colleges and universities would have been subservient to rhetoric and that rhetoric would have emerged as a "general clearing house for ideas," as Hunt once phrased it, in such institutions. In practical terms, no Dean would ever have accepted such an expansive mission for a new department and certainly no faculty committee would approve establishing such a department that would have made all other departments second-class citizens. The tide for organizing higher education and creating academic departments was moving in the opposite direction from the way Hunt wanted to move.

On this issue, the Midwesterners were much more attuned to the realities and politics of early twentieth century higher education. As Woolbert had said in his previous debates with Hunt, where specialization and professionalism were demanded, he would become a specialist and professional. Had Hunt's ideas carried the day in those early days, it is doubtful that, as O'Neill said, departments of speech would be established, and perhaps the ones already in existence would have been abolished.

Indeed, several years later at Swarthmore, Hunt's own department was abolished by President Frank Aydelotte, and Everett was unable to save it. In 1966 the Cornell department—that had been based on many of the ideas first advanced by Hunt and Hudson, Drummond and Wichelns—was itself abolished when it could no longer adapt to the professional demands of other departments or justify what was seen as its lack of a specific field of specialized academic research. And in his later years, Hunt admitted that he had misunderstood the drive for professional recognition and that his ideas about rhetoric would not have achieved such recognition.

As Wichelns remarked, the debate at the 1922 joint convention left the members unmoved. Hunt's "heresy" remained localized at Cornell with a few outposts among his sympathizers elsewhere and later among Cornell graduates who filled positions at other universities. In fact, his heresy was so effectively exorcised that a 1954 Speech Association of America authorized history of the speech profession glossed over this debate and its index contains no mention of Hunt or Hudson or Wichelns.[77] It was not until years after his retirement that Hunt began to gain recognition for his contributions to the field and then mainly and ironically for his specialized work on Greek rhetoric.

But that is not to say that Hunt's all-encompassing vision of rhetoric as an intellectual mission was without value. He added substance to form in public speaking and in all other endeavors, a position that *individual* teachers and scholars, if they were so moved, could use to justify forays into politics, ethics, history, literature, and other fields of knowledge. It was upon such individuals that Hunt had his greatest influence rather than on the profession as a whole or upon those seeking to find ways to get public speaking recognized as a respectable department in other colleges and universities. Perhaps, that's as it should have been. Everett's teaching was always highly individual, preferring conferences with students to lecturing on rules or precepts.

One final result of the 1922 convention needs to be mentioned. Despite his "heresy" Hunt was elected President of the Eastern Public Speaking Conference that year and served a two-year term.

The Full Flowering of Cornell Scholarship

By 1925 the little group at Cornell had achieved stature in the field. The National Association had appointed Alexander Drummond to chair a committee on public speaking for secondary schools and to supervise a report on that subject. Cornellians were conspicuous on the committee and contributed significantly to the final report: Caplan ("Communication The Basic Principle"), Hudson ("The Rhetoric of Spoken Discourse"), Hunt ("The Choice of Subjects for Student Speeches"), Winans ("The Class Hour"), Parrish ("The Use of the Declamation"), Utterback ("The Group Discussion"), Lee Hultzen ("Phonetics and the Teaching of Elocution"), Russell H. Wagner ("Conversational Quality in Delivery") and Drummond ("Dramatics and Speech Training"). James O'Neill, Smiley Blanton, and Charles Woolbert among others also contributed brief sections.[78]

More important was another volume published by the same publishing house in the same year. In 1923 James Winans was diagnosed as having an inoperable cancer. His old friends at Cornell were distressed at the news and became determined to honor Winans. Therefore, under the direction of Drummond and with the assistance of Wichelns and Lee S. Hultzen, they prepared a *festschrift* to pay respects to Winans before he died. Of course, they could not know at the time that the Winans' cancer would eventually abate and he would live on for another quarter of a century. They wrote furiously in the time they had and rushed the volume into print.

Studies in Rhetoric and Public Speaking in Honor of James Albert Winans by his Pupils and Colleagues was published in 1925 in a limited edition of 400 copies, of which Everett's was number 81. The 11 essays—all original works—that made up the volume ranged from a long opening essay on classical rhetoric (Hunt) to a psychological study of argumentation (Utterback), from a theory of rhetorical criticism (Wichelns) to specific examinations of Bacon, De Quincey and Emerson (Hannah, Hudson, and Theodore Stenberg respectively), from a translation of a medieval tractate on preaching (Caplan) to two investigations of stuttering (Smiley Blanton and Margaret Blanton), from the rhythms of oratory (Parrish) to study of phonetics and elocution (Hultzen). It was dedicated to James Albert Winans who "by his work in college classrooms, by his writings, and by his personal qualities . . . has exercised a beneficent leadership in the field of academic instruction in public speaking . . . ."[79]

The two most important pieces in the volume were Wichelns' "The Literary Criticism of Oratory" and Hunt's "Plato and Aristotle on Rhetoric and Rhetoricians," each of which exerted permanent influence within the profession. Since both essays are well-known within the profession, only brief statements about their importance need be noted here. Donald C. Bryant wrote that "The Literary Criticism of Oratory" set the "pattern and determined the direction of rhetorical criticism for more than a quarter of a century and

Everett Lee Hunt and Wilbur Samuel Howell identified 11 of the 15 early ECA members in the photograph above. The photograph was taken in 1922 in Ithaca, New York. Many were on the faculty at Cornell. The 11 persons whose identities have been established are (1) Robert Hannah, (2) Everett Lee Hunt, ECA President, 1923-24; (5) William E. Utterback; (6) Alexander M. Drummond; (8) Herbert A. Wichelns, ECA President, 1931; (9) Howard A. Bradley; (10) Wayland Maxfield Parrish, ECA President, 1934-35; (11) Harry Caplan; (12) Hoyt H. Hudson, ECA President, 1929-30; (13) Marvin G. Bauer, ECA Secretary-Treasurer, 1947-48, ECA President, 1954; and (15) Russell H. Wagner, ECA President, 1948.

has had a greater and more continuous influence upon the development of the scholarship of rhetoric and public address than any other single work published in this century."[80] What distinguished Wichelns' conception of rhetorical criticism from other forms of criticism was not method or system, but "point of view."[81] Nonetheless, other scholars soon developed methods and a system from Wichelns' original essay, the fullest expression of that system being Thonssen and Baird's *Speech Criticism* and the most extensive applications of his "method" in the three volumes of *History and Criticism of American Public Address.*[82] In subsequent years Wichelns did not produce any work comparable to this essay and privately he bemoaned that his ideas had been misunderstood.[83] Indeed, he directed the study that made the most thorough-going attack on the institutionalization of Wichelns' original ideas: Black's *Rhetorical Criticism: A Study in Method.*

Hunt's "Plato and Aristotle on Rhetoric and Rhetoricians" was the most impressive and sustained piece of scholarship published in the first two decades of the profession. If it is not the definitive word on classical Greek rhetoric, it remains an indispensible study that any scholar who came to the same subject afterwards had to acknowledge and master even if he or she disagreed with Hunt. The long essay contained Hunt's sympathetic survey of the various sophists, his delineation of Plato's attacks on rhetoric as well as Plato's conception of a "true" rhetoric, his description of Aristotle's answers to Plato and his summary of the main points of Aristotelian rhetoric. The publication of his essay established Hunt as a formidable scholar in his own right with many of the credentials necessary to speak with authority on academic and educational matters. (In later years Everett would urge young academics—me, in particular—to publish a major but specialized work in order to establish such credentials as preparation for writing what one really wanted to write.)

But "Plato and Aristotle" was more than distinguished scholarship. The opening line was pure Everett Hunt and applied directly to him: "The art of rhetoric offered to the Athenian of the fifth century B.C. a method of higher education and, beyond that, a way of life."[84] For Everett, rhetoric was truly a method of higher education, as he had repeatedly stated in his arguments with Woolbert and O'Neill. Among the ancient Greeks he found an intellectual base and tradition for his view of a modern conception of rhetoric and public speaking:

> In the problems of the relations of Plato to Protogoras, of philosopher to sophist and rhetoricians, are involved the issues which we debate when we discuss the aims of a liberal education, the desirability of government by experts, the relations of a university to the state, the duty of a scholar in a democracy, the function of public opinion in a popular government, the difference between a conventional and a rational morality, to say nothing of more speculative questions.

The Greeks had long before raised "persistent questions for public discussion" and had relied on rhetoric as one means for addressing them. Thus, studying the best of what they had thought would assist in provoking the best that teachers and students could think. His study, then, of Greek rhetoric was not a dry philological study of limited historical value, but a living testament and guide for modern rhetoricians who would apply their own imagination and intellect to contemporary problems.

Beyond that, rhetoric was a way of life. Everett saw life rhetorically, and it was the Greek idea of rhetoric that guided him. In this sense, he could be mistaken for some of the post-modern literary and rhetorical theorists. But unlike them his key word for unlocking his vision of rhetoric was not *persuasion* or *identification*, but *probability*. Hunt eschewed certainty in life and found little in common with those who sought certainty. He was interested in public issues that resided in the realm of probability, significant issues about which people debate and which they must decide through participation in political and civic life. His emphasis on ideas within the realm of probability accounts for his disdain of specialized scholarship that searched for the facts and his persistent criticism of science (be it natural, physical or social science) that sought certainty. Discovering facts did not tell him anything significant about how to conceive of or relate to the ideas he wished to conceive of and relate to. Instead, it would take all the knowledge a human could accumulate and all the wisdom and imagination one could muster to wrestle mightily with public questions on enduring issues. The idea that rhetoric was based on probabilities led Hunt to develop a humane rhetoric. Such a rhetoric required one to explore ideas with imagination, to express them with intelligence, and to view opposing opinions with sympathy. And it is this emphasis on sympathy for the opinions of others that certainly separates his ideas from those of postmodern cultural and marxist critics. Such was his view of a humane rhetoric and a humane life.

Furthermore, Hunt saw the potential for power in rhetoric. But again unlike some postmodern theorists, he did not see power in terms of dominance and submission. His respect for tradition and his innate sense of Christian civility prohibited that. As he wrote in a later essay, each generation will "see their own truths, will pass away, be scoffed at, and finally . . will have some small part of their judgments accepted as belonging to the wisdom of the ages."[85] He would be satisfied with that.

Studies in Rhetoric and Public Speaking was a landmark book. Reviewing its original publication, James O'Neill stated: "The work is of great professional interest, first, because we have not had anything like it before. It is not a textbook, but a volume of scholarly papers for teachers and scholars of the profession."[86] O'Neill quickly noted the three most distinguished essays—Hunt's "Plato and Aristotle," Wichelns "Literary Criticism of Oratory," and Caplan's "A Late Medieval Tractate"—and observed that the others were "less brilliant achievements" when compared to these "pre-eminent examples of interesting and scholarly additions to the literature of our field."[87] He predicted that teachers would direct their future graduate students to these studies not only as examples of contemporary scholarship but as standards to aspire to. O'Neill concluded his long ten-page review by describing the book as a "distinguished achievement," the "most significant volume offered to workers in the field of speech in a very, very long time."[88]

Hunt Leaves Cornell

By 1925 when *Studies in Rhetoric and Public Speaking* was published, the small band at Cornell had created an impressive record. Little doubt that they were the dominant group in the new profession that now celebrated its eleventh anniversary. Winans had published the most popular and distinguished textbook of the period, a book that Thonssen and Baird later described as "the greatest contribution to rhetorical theory since George Campbell's *Philosophy of Rhetoric*."[89] Hunt and Drummond had edited *Persistent Questions in Public Discussion* that gave "substance to form" in public speaking classes. The two professors had inaugurated the first graduate seminar in classical rhetoric in the twentieth-century and set a precedent for all other graduate programs so that no reputable department would dare neglect the subject, regardless of what emphasis or importance it gave to the ancients. Caplan and Cooper had begun translating ancient and medieval rhetorical treatises so that they could be made readily available to scholars and students alike. Hudson had defined the field of rhetoric and given persuasive arguments for distinguishing rhetorical studies from literary studies in his "Rhetoric and Poetry." Wichelns had established a perspective for rhetorical criticism that would dominate the next two generations of rhetorical critics. Hunt had examined the intellectual foundations for rhetoric and had broadened and given humane depth to those foundations. Together the scholarly works of this company of Cornellians contributed to academic respectability for the new profession and brought distinction to themselves both as a group and individually.

But at the very time of their triumph, they were also breaking up. Winans had already departed for Dartmouth. Drummond was turning his attention to his first love, drama. Hudson had graduated and gone off to Swarthmore. Caplan left public speaking to join the Classics department. Cooper remained in the English department but would soon become a one man department of Comparative Literature. Wichelns had left after the original seminar to follow Winans to Dartmouth and then on the Pittsburgh, only to return to Cornell in 1924. And then there was Hunt.

Why did Hunt leave Cornell at the zenith of the original group's fame? The answers were both personal and professional.

In 1964, almost 40 years later, there was a vacancy at Cornell and Hal Harding urged me to apply for it. Before doing so I journeyed out to Swarthmore to ask Everett's opinion. He counselled against it. It was one of the few times I heard him speak critically of his colleagues from the Cornell days. He said he had been unhappy there because of the atmosphere. Winans had hassled him about his teaching. His best friend, Hudson, had left in 1923. Among those left, Cooper was too authoritarian, Wichelns—though brilliant—too gloomy and pessimistic, and Caplan, a genial story-teller, was more interested in specialized scholarship and translations than ideas. I got the distinct impression that his years at Cornell were not happy years. When Mrs. Hunt gave me his papers, I found an almost complete record of his undergraduate days at Huron, but virtually nothing from his days at Cornell.

More important, Cornell was a dead-end for Hunt. He was now 35 years old, and he was ambitious. But he did not have a Ph.D. and had no way of getting one from another university since Ithaca was so far removed from other universities that granted advanced degrees. He was told that he could take graduate courses at Cornell, but he would have to be demoted to the rank of instructor with a reduction of his salary by one-half. Hunt could not financially afford that what with his wife and his family to support. (In addition to normal expenses, he was supporting his sister, Genevieve, who was attending Ithaca College.) Attempting to pursue the doctorate during summers, as he had for his Master's, would be a long and difficult task. Therefore, he found himself in a dilemma. He could not advance professionally at Cornell because he did not have a doctorate, and he could not get a doctorate at Cornell without assuming a major financial burden. The only way out was to leave. But where to go?

By a stroke of good fortune, Hoyt Hudson, who was at Swarthmore, received an offer at about this time from the University of Pittsburgh that included a raise in salary and a promotion to full Professor in the English Department. He took it and recommended Hunt as his replacement.

So, Hunt journeyed down from Ithaca to the little village of Swarthmore where the small Quaker college was located. There he met with President Aydelotte and his committee. They offered him an attractive position in public speaking, the largest department on campus. They offered to almost double his salary from $ 2,500 to $ 4,000. They said he could do graduate work in Philadelphia at the University of Pennsylvania. Hunt asked for a little time to consider their offer and went out of the meeting to sit under a sycamore tree to think it over.

He later said that he was torn in several directions. Leaving Cornell for Swarthmore would mean leaving a university for a college, leaving a graduate department to teach undergraduates. But until he earned a doctorate there was little chance for teaching graduate courses and no chance for advancement at Ithaca. The opportunities at Swarthmore, including its proximity to the University of Pennsylvania, seemed the best opportunity available to this ambitious young scholar.

What also influenced him was Aydelotte's enthusiasm for quality education and the Quaker atmosphere on campus. President Aydelotte had embarked on revolutionizing undergraduate education, and Swarthmore was his experiment. He was filled with ideas and enthusiasm for instituting them. He wanted to de-emphasize the "sideshows" of college life (athletics and extracurricular activities) and promote the "main tent" (intellectual pursuits). That impressed Everett although he could not have known at that time what the consequences would be for him. Also, it should be remembered that Everett was deeply religious. There were Nantucket Quakers among his ancestors, and he had always had more inclinations toward the Friends than toward Calvinism. After what must have been some lengthy soul-searching, he decided to accept the offer.

His tenure at Cornell came to an end at the end of the 1924-25 school year, and he left Ithaca to embark upon a new adventure in education.

Notes

[1] Morris Bishop, "And Perhaps Cornell," *Our Cornell* (Ithaca: Cornell Alumni Association, 1939, reissued in 1947), p. 61.

[2] Carl L. Becker, *Cornell University: Founders and the Founding* (Ithaca: Cornell University Press, 1944), p. 197.

[3] Raymond F. Howes, "E.B. Titchener," *A Cornell Notebook* (Ithaca: Cornell Alumni Association, 1971), pp. 41-49. See, also: Howes, "Notes on E.B. Titchener," *Important To Me* (privately printed, Riverside, 1980), pp. 1-18. Howes was Titchener's nephew.

[4] Morris Bishop, *A History of Cornell* (Ithaca: Cornell University Press, 1962).

[5] Twenty-year-olds were given a three month course, the nineteen-year-olds a six-month course, and eighteen-year-olds a full nine-month course. These courses were a mixture of military training and regular university courses useful for future officers. See: Bishop, pp. 429-431.

[6] Bishop, p. 430.

[7] Bishop, p. 394.

[8] Bishop, p. 472.

[9] Bishop, p. 444.

[10] Denis Condon, *The Foundations of the Cornell School of Rhetoric*, unpublished Ph.D. dissertation (Pittsburgh: University of Pittsburgh, 1988), p. 101. For additional details about Cooper's life, see pp. 100-108.

[11] Lane Cooper, *Experiments in Education* (Ithaca: Cornell University Press, 1943), p.84.

[12] Taped interview with Everett Lee Hunt by Windt, August 10, 1967.

[13] Condon, pp. 139-145.

[14] Lane Cooper, "Patterns," *Two Views of Education* (New Haven: Yale University Press, 1922), p. 147.

[15] Cooper, "Teacher and Student," *Two Views of Education*, p. 138.

[16] Cooper, "The Function of the Leader in Scholarship," *Two Views of Education*, p. 193.

[17] Hunt, taped recorded interview with Windt.

[18] Cited by Condon from Harold W. Thompson, "Alexander M. Drummond," *Hamilton Alumni Review* (January 1936), p. 52.

[19] Donald K. Smith, "Development of Departments of Speech," *A History of Speech Education in America*, Ed. by Karl Wallace (New York: Appleton-Century-Crofts, 1954), p. 460.

[20] *Ibid.*, pp. 460-461.

[21] Hoyt H. Hudson, "Alexander M. Drummond," *Studies in Speech and Drama In Honor of Alexander M. Drummond* (Ithaca: Cornell University Press, 1944), pp. 3-4.

[22] *Ibid.*, p. 5.

[23] For a sampling of considerations of his importance, see: Giles Wilkeson Gray, "Some Teachers and the Transition to Twentieth-Century Speech Education," in *A History of Speech Education in America*, pp. 433-436; Alexander M. Drummond, "James A. Winans, '97," *Hamilton Alumni Review*, 4 (1939), p. 89; Loren Reid, "James Albert Winans (1872-1956), *Southern Speech Communication Journal*, 31 (Winter 1982), pp. 89-117; Carroll C. Arnold, "Rhetoric in America Since 1900," *Re-establishing the "Speech Profession: The First Fifty Years*, Ed. by Robert T. Oliver and Marvin G. Bauer (No place of publication specified: Speech Association of the Eastern States, September 1959); Herbert H. Wichelns, *A History of the Speech Association of the Eastern States* (No place of publication specified: Speech Association of the Eastern States, September 1959); Molly Wertheimer, "Attention and Other Useful Notions from William James's Work," paper delivered in honor of James Winans at the 1989 Speech Communication Association annual meeting, San Francisco, CA.

[24] Address at the Commemorative Meeting of the Speech [Communication] Association in 1957, as quoted in Howes, "Tributes to James A. Winans," in *Notes on the Cornell School of Rhetoric*, pp. 7.

[26] Quoted in Condon (p. 82) from Waterman Thomas Hewett, *Cornell University: A History* (New York: The University Publishing Society, 1905), p. 58.

[27] James M. O'Neill, review of *Public Speaking* by James Albert Winans, in *Quarterly Journal of Public Speaking*, 2 (April 1916), pp. 213-215.

[28] Loren Reid, "James Albert Winans (1872-1956)," p. 116.

[29] Drummond, "James Albert Winans '97," p. 90.

[30] Note from Alan Hunt to Windt, November 29, 1989.

[31] Xeroxed copies of course offering in Public Speaking Department for the school years, 1918-1919 and 1919-1920.

[32] Hoyt H. Hudson, "Alexander M. Drummond," p. 4.

[33] Everett Lee Hunt, "The Cornell School of Humane Rhetoric," unpublished three page manuscript written at the request of Windt, 1981, p. 1.

[34] *Ibid.*

[35] Everett Lee Hunt, "Herbert A. Wichelns and the Cornell Tradition of Rhetoric as a Humane Subject," *The Rhetorical Idiom*, Ed. by Donald C. Bryant (Ithaca: Cornell University Press, 1958).

[36] From a letter by Everett Lee Hunt in "Addresses delivered at the Meeting Honoring Professor Harry Caplan at the convention of the Speech Association of America," Statler Hilton Hotel, New York City, December 30, 1965, edited by John F. Wilson and published by the Department of Speech and Drama, Cornell University, n.p.

[37] Bishop, *A History of Cornell*, p. 404.

[38] See the letter from Charles E. Bennett dated March 27, 1919 in Harry Caplan's files in the Cornell Archives which Condon cites in his dissertation.

[39] See Condon's "The Foundations of the Cornell School of Rhetoric," pp. 120-122.

[40] Helen North, Memorial for Harry Caplan ("Quis Desiderio Sit Pudor Aut Modus Tam Cari Capitis?", December 5, 1980.

[41] About Wichelns' problems at the University of Pittsburgh, see: Raymond F. Howes, "Herbert A. Wichelns and the Study of Rhetoric," *Notes on the Cornell School of Rhetoric*, p. 14.

[42] Hunt, "Herbert A. Wichelns and the Cornell Tradition of Rhetoric as a Humane Study," p. 1.

[43] Hudson, "Alexander M. Drummond," p. 4.

[44] Herbert A. Wichelns, "A History of the Speech Association of the Eastern States," p. 7

[45] Donald C. Bryant, "The Founders of the Cornell Tradition of Rhetorical Study," a paper presented at the Speech Association of America convention, 1957, p.6.

[46] Hudson, "Alexander M. Drummond," p. 4.

[47] Herbert A. Wichelns, "A History of the Speech Association of the Eastern States," published by the Speech Association of the Eastern States (April, 1959), p. 7.

[48] Hunt, "Creative Teaching in War Time," *Quarterly Journal of Speech Education*, 4 (October 1918), p. 386.

[49] *Ibid.*, p. 397.

[50] Wilber Samuel Howell, "Everett Hunt at Cornell: A Personal Recollection," a two page letter sent to Windt, November 4, 1989.

[51] Raymond F. Howes, Notes on the Cornell School of Rhetoric, p. 10.

[52] "Studies in Rhetoric" found among Hunt's papers and now in the possession of Ted Windt by permission of Mrs. Hunt.

[53] Some notes come from the Cornell days because his handwriting in those days is identifiable. Everett wrote in a small hand and his writing became progressively more crabbed as the years passed, even to the point that it is indecipherable except to the most trained student of his handwriting. Other notes were added when he was at Swarthmore because some notes are written on the back of notices about faculty meetings, such as the one dated February 27, 1930.

[54] C. Harold King, "This Man, Hunt," paper read by Carroll Arnold at the 1959 Speech Association of America convention panel honoring Everett Lee Hunt on his retirement, December 18, 1959, p. 1.

[55] *Ibid.*, p. 11.

[56] Howell, "Everett Lee Hunt at Cornell: A Personal Recollection," p. 2. Howes recalled this same incident in his brief piece on Everett in Notes on the Cornell School of Rhetoric, p. 11.

[57] Howes, Notes on the Cornell School of Rhetoric, p. 11.

[58] Hunt, from the tape recording of the seminar at Temple University, 1971.

[59] John Dolman, Jr., review of Persistent Questions in Public Discussion in *Quarterly Journal of Speech Education*, 9 (November 1924), p. 396.

[60] *Classified Models of Speech Composition*, compiled by James Milton O'Neill (New York: The Century Company, 1922), p. ix.

[61] "Preface," *Persistent Questions in Public Discussion*, ed. by Alexander M. Drummond and Everett Lee Hunt (New York: The Century Co., 1924), p. v.

[62] Hunt, "A Word to Teachers," *Persistent Questions*, p. 486.

[63] Hunt, "The Scientific Spirit in Public Speaking," p. 193.

[64] Among these were: W. P. Sanford, "The Problems of Speech Content," *Quarterly Journal of Speech Education*, 8 (November 1922), pp. 364-371; James M. O'Neill, "Speech Content and Course Content," *Quarterly Journal of Speech Education*, 9 (February 1923), pp. 25-52: James Winans, "Speech," *Quarterly Journal of Speech Education*, 9 (June, 1923), pp. 223-231; Herbert A. Wichelns, "Our Hidden Aims," *Quarterly Journal of Speech Education*, 9 (November 1923), pp. 315-323; W.P. Sandford, "Content and Form," *Quarterly Journal of Speech Education*, 9 (November 1923), pp. 324-329; E.C. Mabie, "'Speech' From Another Angle," *Quarterly Journal of Speech Education*, 9 (November 1923), pp. 330-333; William H. Davis, "Courses for the Few or the Many," *Quarterly Journal of Speech Education*, 9 (November 1923), pp. 358-362.

[65] Hunt, "Adding Substance to Form in Public Speaking Courses," *Quarterly Journal of Speech Education*, 8 (1922), p. 257.

[66] James M. O'Neill, "Speech Content and Course Content in Public Speaking," *Quarterly Journal of Speech Education, 9* (1923), p. 27.

[67] *Ibid.*

[68] *Ibid.*, p. 30.

[69] Hunt, "Knowledge and Skill," *Quarterly Journal of Speech Education, 9* (February 1923), p. 69.

[70] *Ibid.*

[71] Hunt, "Knowledge and Skill," pp. 70-71.

[72] Herbert A. Wichelns, "A History of the Speech Association of the Eastern States," published by the Speech Association of the Eastern States (1959), p. 7.

[73] Hoyt H. Hudson, "The Field of Rhetoric," *Quarterly Journal of Speech Education, 9* (April 1923), p. 180.

[74] Alexander M. Drummond, "Graduate Work in Public Speaking," pp. 136-146 and "Some Subjects for Graduate Study—Department of Public Speaking, Cornell University," pp 147-153, both published in the April 1923 issue of the *Quarterly Journal of Speech Education.*

[75] Review by Loren Reid of *The Rhetorical Idiom: Essays in Rhetoric, Oratory, Language and Drama Presented to Herbert August Wichelns,* Edited by Donald C. Bryant (Ithaca: Cornell University Press, 1958) in *Quarterly Journal of Speech, 44* (October 1958), pp. 31-317.

[76] Donald C. Bryant, "The Founders of the Cornell Tradition of Rhetorical Study."

[77] Karl Wallace, Ed., *A History of Speech Education in America* (New York: Appleton-Century-Crofts, 1954), pp. 503-504.

[78] Alexander M. Drummond, *A Course of Study in Speech Training and Public Speaking for Secondary Schools* (New York: The Century Co., 1925).

[79] Dedication page' *Studies in Rhetoric and Public Speaking in Honor of James Albert Winans by Pupils and Colleagues* (New York: The Century Co., 1925).

[80] Donald C. Bryant, *The Rhetorical Idiom,* p. 5.

[81] Donald C. Bryant, *Rhetorical Dimensions in Criticism* (Baton Rouge: Louisiana State University, 1973), p. 28.

[82] Lester Thonssen and A. Craig Baird, *Speech Criticism* (New York: Ronald Press, 1948); William Norwood Brigance, Ed., *A History of American Public Address,* Vols. I & II (New York: McGraw-Hill Book Company, Inc., 1943); and Marie Kathryn Hochmuth [Nichols], Ed., *History and Criticism of American Public Address,* Vol. III (London: Longmans, Green, 1955).

[83] See Edwin Black, "Herbert A. Wichelns and Effects," paper delivered in honor of Wichelns at the annual meeting of the Speech Communication Association, San Francisco, CA, 1989.

[84] Hunt, "Plato and Aristotle on Rhetoric and Rhetoricians," p. 3.

[85] Hunt, "Matthew Arnold and His Critics," *Sewanee Review, 44* (October-December 1936), p. 467.

[86] James M. O'Neill, "New Books," review of *Studies in Rhetoric and Public Speaking in Honor of James Albert Winans, Quarterly Journal of Speech Education, 11* (November 1926), p. 368.

[87] *Ibid.*, p. 369.

[88] *Ibid.*, p. 377.

[89] Thonssen and Baird, *Speech Criticism,* p. 144.

4

Settling in at Swarthmore

The Swarthmore College that Everett Hunt joined in 1925 was a college on the brink of an education revolution. It had been founded in 1864 by the Hicksite branch of the Religious Society of Friends. The wealthier Orthodox branch of Quakers had established Haverford in 1833, but Hicksite Friends did not believe it to be an appropriate institution for their children. So they located their institution in rural Delaware County outside Philadelphia and named it Swarthmore after Swarthmoor Hall, which had been the English home of Margaret Fell, the Mother of Quakerism and wife of George Fox, the founder of the Religious Society of Friends.[1] Richard Walton observed:

> The Quakers were far behind the other Protestant denominations in the establishment of colleges, and the reasons were simple. The other Protestants were evangelistic, seeking to enlarge their flocks. For that they needed growing numbers of educated ministers. The Quakers did not believe in proselytizing, nor did they believe in ordained ministers. They believed that men and women came to and remained with the Society because of an "inner light" that required no recruitment, no professional ministers, and not even much in the way of education. It is a nice paradox that Swarthmore, now known for its intellectual rigor, and other fine Quaker colleges were founded by a sect that was not primarily known for its intellectual pursuits.[2]

As "guarded" (from outside influences) as the college was supposed to be, Swarthmore was also progressive from the beginning in a variety of areas. It was co-educational, offered some electives, and placed more emphasis on science than other institutions of higher education. Its first class (4 men and 1 woman) included Helen Magill, daughter of the second president of Swarthmore, who went on to become the first woman in the United States to earn a Ph.D.[3]

In his book, *The Revolt of the College Intellectual*, Hunt described three different periods in the development of Swarthmore's history up to 1962: "the early period, in which the religious purposes of the founders were dominant in keeping the college apart from the world; a middle period, which reflected the prevailing values and mores of the time and in which the college was in and of the world; and a third period, in which intellectual values gained dominance and which some critics have called the period of eggheads in the nest."[4] The first period is self-explanatory. The second occurred around the turn of the century when student social activities and athletics began to dominate the life of the college. Swarthmore was a big time football school playing such other powers as Pennsylvania and Princeton. The tuition bills of some players were paid by alumni, the school boasted some 62 student organizations (for a population of 400 students), and Swarthmore gained a reputation as an "educational country club."[5] The College seemed to exemplify Woodrow Wilson's famous remark about colleges of that era that the side-shows were swallowing up the main circus. But all of that was to change after World War I. And the major reason for that change was one man, the man who brought Hunt to Swarthmore: Frank Aydelotte.

Frank Aydelotte (1880-1956) was born in Sullivan, Indiana to a prosperous family. He received his B.A. from Indiana University, worked as a reporter, English instructor, football coach, and eventually earned his M.A. in English at Harvard. But what was crucial in the development of his educational philosophy were the three years he spent at Oxford.

Aydelotte won a Rhodes scholarship in 1905, and spent his years at Oxford earning a B.Litt. Returning to the United States, he became an outspoken advocate of the Oxford system of education and a persistent critic of mediocrity in American higher education. From 1914 to 1921 he was editor of the *American Oxonian*, and in 1917 he became American secretary of the Rhodes Scholarship Trust. He taught first at Indiana University and then at the Massachusetts Institute of Technology as Professor of English. All the while though he was pressing for higher intellectual standards in colleges and universities. Above all, he wanted to institute the Oxford system, and he began looking for a suitable place to try out his British experiment in one American college. In 1921 he got his opportunity when Swarthmore offered him its presidency, and he persuaded faculty and trustees to institute an Honors program. In his presidential inaugural address, Aydelotte set forth his ambitions for superior students and outlined his plan for the honors program. But let Hunt summarize the innovations Aydelotte brought to the Quaker school:

> And when he selected Swarthmore, a small rural Quaker college, as the best place to try to create an equivalent of the Oxford atmosphere in America, he was sure that the small college had the best means of mobilizing student interests around intellectual concerns. He helped to intellectualize the 'peer culture.' And he did, with some surprising results. What has happened at Swarthmore since he became president . . . has been described by outside observers as "controlled metamorphosis."[6]

The "metamorphosis" did not occur overnight. Aydelotte had enthusiastic supporters, but he also met with resistance, especially when he de-emphasized athletics. At first, it was only an experiment to be reviewed after several years. In fact, it would take almost a decade to bend the college to his vision of a truly intellectual campus.

To make it intellectual meant not only recruiting outstanding students but also outstanding faculty. In the first decade Richard Walton noted that Aydelotte recruited, among others: Mary Albertson, the medieval historian; Edith Philips, the French scholar; Bland Blanshard, later to become president of the American Philosophical Association; Lucius Rogers Shero, the classics scholar; and Everett Lee Hunt, whose "reputation in academic circles was matched by his influence as teacher of English literature and dean of the College."[7] If Walton was not certain about exactly how Everett had achieved his academic reputation, he at least recognized him as one of the people who would become an influential member of the distinguished faculty Aydelotte was assembling.

Aydelotte served as President from 1921 to 1940, the years in which Swarthmore was transformed. He left to become the second director of the Institute for Advanced Study at Princeton, a position he unhappily held until his retirement in 1947 when he was succeeded by J. Robert Oppenheimer. But this is getting ahead of our story. Suffice it to say that in 1925 when Hunt arrived at Swarthmore the changes were just underway.

From Public Speaking to Literary Criticism, 1925-1933

The Department of Public Speaking that Hunt inherited from Hoyt Hudson was the largest department on campus in 1925. It had been built up by Paul M. ("Pops") Pearson, father of the journalist Drew Pearson. The elder Pearson (1871-1938) had taken over the department in 1902 and continued as its driving force until 1923 when Hudson succeeded him. Pearson was also a major force in the creation of the Public Speaking Conference of the New England and the North Atlantic States (now called the Eastern Communication Association). In 1910 Wilbur Jones Kay, James Winans and Pearson had joined their forces to establish what was to become the oldest continuing professional organization for teachers of speech. The new Conference's first meeting was held in April, 1910 at Swarthmore.

Over the next ten years or so Pearson's energies were diverted more and more to the Swarthmore Chautauqua that he founded in 1912. Around the time of World War I Swarthmore became more active on the Chautauqua circuit, even introducing the first Junior Program. At the height of its touring, the Swarthmore Chautauqua visited nearly one thousand towns annually in 14 Eastern states and in three Canadian provinces.[8] Although the Chautauqua had no official connection with the College, it had a direct effect on the Public Speaking department. Students quickly learned that summer jobs were available to them as crewpersons or Junior Leaders on the circuit. Taking courses or majoring in public speaking would do no great harm to their chances of getting one of these prized summer jobs. Thus, by the time Pearson resigned from Swarthmore to give his full attention to the Chautauqua in 1923, the Department of Public Speaking was the largest department on campus and still was when Hunt joined the faculty as Acting Assistant Professor of Public Speaking.

Even though his first year was marred by the death of his father (October 29, 1925), Hunt quickly found a home in Swarthmore. Perhaps, it was a return to another small town and small college such as the ones he had grown up in; perhaps, it was the vibrant department that he would head; perhaps, it was the opportunity finally to pursue studies toward his doctorate; perhaps, it was the spiritual home he found, for at Swarthmore, he shook loose his Presbyterianism and joined the Religious Society of Friends.

Hunt had been introduced to his religious heritage while visiting his maternal grandparents in Fountain City, Indiana when he was still a child. John Wright Johnson, his grandfather who had become a Quaker when he married his third wife, was a nephew of Levi Coffin, the founder of the underground railroad. He was associated with his uncle in helping slaves escape and was proud that he had talked with Eliza Harris, the internationally famous "Eliza crossing the ice" in Harriet Beecher Stowe's *Uncle Tom's Cabin*.[9] Of course, on the Hunt side, there had been Nantucket Quakers among his ancestors, and his family had a long history within the Friends. But there had been a break in that tradition. Oral family history has it that one of Hunt's ancestors had been "read out of meeting" from the Friends because he had trimmed his beard in violation of strict Quaker dictums. Another story said that Hunt's father rebelled against the Quaker heritage by becoming a fundamentalist minister.[10] (Usually Hunt gave this version when talking about his father.) Whatever the case, Hunt found in the Hicksite Meeting on the College grounds a place of intellectual excitement as well as of Friendly dedication, and he remained an active member and participant until his death. And the Quaker combination of reverent individualism and of committed social action was a combination truly in accord with his own beliefs.

During his first years at Swarthmore Hunt flourished. Philip M. Hicks, the other professor in the department, was chiefly responsible for drama courses and would remain Hunt's colleague until Hicks' retirement in 1953. Hicks was to become one of the college's best loved teachers so that even the "eyes of old grads light up when his name is mentioned."[11] He was also controversial, at least to the world outside Swarthmore. In the 1940s he appeared as a witness in the obscenity trial over James T. Farrell's *Studs Lonigan* novels testifying for the defense about the artistic merits of Farrell's work. In the 1950s he opposed McCarthyism and joined with several hundred others in urging the Supreme Court to declare the McCarran Act unconstitutional. Hicks, a life-long bachelor, was known for the legendary parties at his home and at his Chester county farm, so much so that upon his death in 1975 his friends threw a memorial party, rather than a service, in his memory.[12]

Hunt's duties within the department were to teach courses in public speaking, argument, interpretive reading, and extempore speaking. He coached debate and administered the College prizes given annually for extempore speaking, debating and oratory. He was quickly promoted from Acting Assistant Professor to Professor of Rhetoric and Oratory and given tenure in 1926. At the same time, he began graduate work first at the University of Pennsylvania and later commuted to Columbia University to complete his studies with Charles Sears Baldwin, author of *Ancient Rhetoric and Poetic* (1924), *Medieval Rhetoric and Poetic* (1928), and *Renaissance Literary Theory and Practice* (1939, edited by Donald Lemen Clark after Baldwin's death in 1936). Everett began translating and writing a commentary on the fourth book of St. Augustine's *De Doctrina Christiana* as his doctoral thesis.

In addition, the National Association named Hunt as editor of the *Quarterly Journal* in 1927 for a three year term. He assigned his good friend, Hoyt Hudson as book review editor. It was during Hunt's tenure that the current name of the journal was finally settled upon. It had begun as the *Quarterly Journal of*

Public Speaking (in deference to the *Public Speaking Review* of which it was an off-shoot), had been changed to the *Quarterly Journal of Speech Education* in 1918, and ten years later was finally re-titled the *Quarterly Journal of Speech.*

Hunt not only edited the journal, but wrote editorials and contributed a great number of book reviews. His maiden editorial set forth his standards but with a typical reassertion of his principal thesis as the head of his priorities:

> It is the function of THE *QUARTERLY JOURNAL OF SPEECH EDUCATION* to present the work of specialists and to aid in the synthesis of the work of specialists. It will discuss matters of taste and temperament that cannot be settled by science and scholarship—that cannot be settled at all. Problems of administration, which as necessary evils bulk so large in American education, cannot be neglected. The exchange of experience and opinion on problems of classroom procedure will always have its place, although the history of academic societies seems to indicate that pedagogical method becomes less absorbing as science and scholarship develop. Contests of one sort and another we still have with us. As long as the management of these is accepted as part of our professional responsibility, questions of method in conducting them will furnish part of our literature. For the present, at least, the *QUARTERLY JOURNAL* must serve as the organ of expression for teachers from the primary grades to the graduate school; it will attempt to do this with the conviction that as much intelligence is required upon one level of the academic hierarchy as another.[13]

The issues Hunt edited did not produce the great number of essays on "taste and temperament that cannot be settled by science or scholarship" that he envisioned as the heart and soul of the profession. And there is an irony in his description of administration, given that he would make his reputation at Swarthmore as an administrator.

The only controversies these years as editor produced were ones Hunt either engaged in or provoked himself. For example, in 1928 he reluctantly published an article on rating scales for public speakers. I say "reluctantly" because Hunt found such precise ratings so obnoxious that he took the liberty of prefacing the article with these words: "The Editor is so prejudiced against rating scales and 'scientific' tests for effective speaking that he has no faith in their value. This article is printed in the hope that it will call forth a general discussion."[14] There was no general discussion in the pages of the *Journal* except for Franklin H. Knower's defense of such scales in his ""Psychological Tests in Public Speaking," (Knower's first publication), and a symposium on "Speech Needs and Objectives Peculiar to Teacher-Training Institutions," both published a year later in the April, 1929 issue.

The April 1928 issue also carried a long editorial by Hunt in response to an address given by Paul Shorey that had been published in *School and Society* in December, 1927.[15] In that address Shorey had attacked certain conceptions of rhetoric and the current purposes for teaching the subject. It was a most peculiar article in that only five years before Shorey had written an admiring article for the *Quarterly Journal* about what contemporary teachers of public speaking could learn from ancient rhetoricians and orators.[16] But now he attacked, and Hunt believed an answer was necessary.

Hunt began with a long quotation from Shorey's address. This excerpt deserves reprinting here because it represents a whole series of attacks on rhetoric that people have made from the times of the ancient Greeks down to today, including even some members of the profession who teach rhetoric. In fact, the charges Shorey made can be heard today especially when journalists and academics decry the manipulation of the public during political campaigns for office. Shorey stated:

> [The domination of ancient democracies by rhetoric is a commonplace of history, but] . . . one of the most amazing illusions of modern optimism is the commonplace that science and critical scholarship have changed all this, that our minds are no longer so easily swayed by rhetoric as were the minds of the ancients. That may be partially true of a few critical and

scientific minds. But man in the mass is still as ever even more a rhetorical animal than he is a political, a logical, or a laughing animal. What deceives us is that tastes in rhetoric change, and certain forms of long-winded, sonorous, old-fashioned bombast no longer appeal to the sophisticated among us. In this sense rhetoric may be defined as the other fellow's fine writing. But if we take rhetoric in its truer and broader sense as a misuse of any kind of fallacy, irrelevance, ornament, emotion, suggestion, wit, epigram, to gain some undue advantage over sober reason and fact, then there never has been a time in the history of mankind when the power of rhetoric was so great . . . . The neglect of such study of rhetoric in our education is very surprising in view of the enormous and increasing part played by public speaking directly, or in report and broadcast, in the formation of that public opinion which is the master of us all. You will perhaps doubt this neglect . . . . What I really mean is not that we don't study rhetoric in a fashion, but that we don't study it in the right way . . . . The dominant aim in all university teaching of these subjects [propaganda and advertisement, and their chief instrument, rhetoric, in all its manifold disguises—*ELH*] should be the establishment of a resisting immunity. It is no legitimate function of public education to teach men how to overreach and overpersuade their fellows. Its proper task is to enlighten and harden the minds of those who make up the staple of audiences against such attempts. I have no time to prove that exploitation is in fact the spirit of our teaching of such subjects as rhetoric, public speaking, psychology, advertising, education, and even history. It is a patent fact . . . .[17]

In his editorial Everett pointed out three weaknesses in Shorey's attack.

First, he noted that Shorey's deprecating definition of rhetoric as the misuse of a variety of techniques and as fallacious reasoning did not include an examination of Shorey's own fallacies and irrelevancies and his misuse of emotion, suggestion, wit and so forth to bolster his contentions. Such a paradox reminded Hunt of another paradox: "Rhetorical argument has always characterized the assailants of rhetoric."

Second, Hunt pointed out the inadequacies of Shorey's call for limiting the teaching of rhetoric to protecting students from its insidious uses: "[I]f we accept Professor Shorey's point of view, and regard the art as an evil, enough comprehension of it to produce immunity might indirectly increase skill in *using* rhetoric, just as a course which aims wholly at producing skill, will indirectly produce a certain amount of resistance to the skill of others. It is as difficult to separate offensive and defensive aspects of rhetoric as it is to distinguish between aggressive and defensive warfare."[18] He compared Shorey's protective approach to Bishop Whately who also believed that people needed to learn the misuses to which rhetoric can be put. But the Bishop, Hunt observed, went beyond such criticisms to transfer his attention from the few who want to acquire rhetorical effectiveness to the many who need to be protected against it: "To do this would be to assume that all rhetorical effectiveness is bad, which would be almost as far from the truth as the assumption that it is altogether good. It would also assume that it is quite possible to impart a critical understanding of an art without any attempt to practise it. To make the study of rhetoric wholly theoretical would be . . . to attempt to build up the immunity he desires without either exercise or inoculation."[19] Such a separation of theory and practice, Hunt believed, would be as pragmatically counter-productive as it would be intellectually stultifying. Hunt would have no part of such easy academic assertions of superiority of theory over practice, elite intellectuals over the mass public, or academic life over public life. These were distinctions that greatly appealed to academics and Shorey had played upon them, but Hunt would have no part of them because he saw them as spurious. He persistently scorned such academic commonplaces in preference for more subtle distinctions that required individual reflection and thought about the quality of particular ideas people presented and the methods by which they advocated them.

Finally, Hunt reproved Shorey for being ignorant of current rhetorical instruction in American colleges and universities. In responding to his assertion that the teaching of rhetoric is intended to "overreach and overpersuade," Hunt concluded that, with the exception of debating and speaking contests, Shorey was "in need of further information."[20] Hunt went on to defend the current leaders of the profession as well as their texts and scholarship.

But Hunt could not end his editorial on the defensive. He continued on to reiterate his own themes. He contended that a comprehensive study of American oratory should be aimed at understanding "its relationship to public opinion in America" and should "make for a more intelligent hearing and reading of the public address of a student's own days as a citizen."[21] But, he lamented, teachers were so preoccupied with the routine of training speakers that they had paid little attention to this goal and thus had produced little rhetorical criticism worth notice. He stated with clarity his own aim: "Critical and analytical study of rhetoric and oratory should not be limited to those who expect to become professional speakers or writers, or to those who expect to teach; it should be offered to all students who desire to understand the significance of rhetoric in modern life."[22] That, indeed, was his aim: to understand the significance of rhetoric in modern life, that is, to understand how public persuasion worked or did not work in the service of ideas and people. But he wanted to do so without self-righteousness or moralizing: "Not too much moral uplift should be demanded of such instruction, nor should it be made too rigidly righteous; more is to be expected from the wide publicity given rhetorical artifice than from the effects of the moral indignation of the teacher."[23]

I have lingered on this editorial for such a time because it represents certain important aspects of Everett's thinking and personality. He wrote it to defend the dignity of rhetoric as a force in education and in a democratic society. He saw rhetoric as central in the modern world and he wanted it humanely studied and practiced. Thus, he responded to Shorey who he believed had given a restricted definition of rhetoric and then attacked this version. Moreover, Hunt responded without rancor or outraged self-righteousness, but with a force and a sweet reasonableness that was informed by a recognition that these were his opinions not universal truths written on tablets from Mt. Sinai. Any other rhetorical stance would have never occurred to him. At the same time, he would not retreat from stating his beliefs (or prejudices, as he often preferred to call them) forthrightly. And in a subsequent issue, Hunt published an article, "Mere Rhetoric," by V.E. Simrell that was an extension of Hunt's defense of rhetoric against Shorey.[24]

Hunt's first several years at Swarthmore were halcyon days, as he recalled to the 50th reunion of the class of 1928.[25] He had successfully completed his tenure as editor of the *Quarterly Journal*, and had become a highly respected member of his profession. He was actively engaged in working on his dissertation. At Swarthmore it was a time of romantic individualism, of vigorous intellectual pursuits and academic change supported by a sustaining tradition from the past. He was at the top of his career. But that was all to change abruptly.

Nineteen twenty-nine was a critical turning point in Hunt's career. First, his dream of earning his doctorate dissolved. He was about half-way through his dissertation that summer when Professor Baldwin informed him that Sister Marie Therese had just published her own translation of St. Augustine's fourth book of *De Doctrina Christiana* and "that the subject was therefore no longer acceptable" to Baldwin.[26] At this point, Hunt gave up pursuing a doctorate. He had worked long and hard on his translation. He was now 39 years old and a tenured full Professor at Swarthmore so he just "said to hell with grad work."[27]

The frustration that Hunt felt must have been exacerbated by a second even more dramatic change in his academic life. As the first experimental period to Oxfordize Swarthmore was coming to an end, Aydelotte redoubled his efforts. Already sports were being de-emphasized and the Honors program was accelerating. But more money was needed to attract faculty and to provide for an appropriate intellectual atmosphere for Aydelotte's British ideas to flourish. In 1929, the first year of the Depression, he embarked upon an audacious endowment campaign to raise almost three million dollars to carry out his educational experiment. The campaign was extended to the next year and was successful in getting more than four million dollars in subscriptions from alumni and foundations. Aydelotte's experiment would not only continue, it would become the defining feature of Swarthmore's reputation for intellectual excellence.

However, the by-product of this surge was that the Department of Public Speaking was abolished and all its courses as well as freshman composition, dramatics, and a variety of other activities. Hunt wrote: "But these activities were [carried on] outside the curriculum; within the community he insisted on rigorous, integrated intellectual work. He did not feel that writing sonnets or singing Bach or producing plays [or debating or teaching public speaking] gained much from attempts to equate them with Latin and Mathematics. In a small college with a faculty cooperating in writing, acting, singing, it was not necessary to subject these pursuits to the grade book."[28] Later, Hunt told me that Aydelotte said that any student intellectually qualified to attend Swarthmore already must know how to speak and write or else that student would not be suitable to be admitted to the College. Given Aydelotte's beliefs, courses in public speaking and written composition were superfluous. In the future any deficiencies in speaking or writing would be handled by tutors. The 1934 catalogue stated: "Students who are reported by any member of the College faculty as deficient in written English are given tutorial guidance for the removal of the deficiency. Written work in courses and in honors seminars takes the place of advanced courses in composition. Study organizations and informal groups for practice in creative writing, acting drama, extempore speaking and debating meet with members of the English Department."[29]

Apparently as a concession to Hunt, one course in public speaking was transferred to the English Department and was only removed from the catalogue while Everett was on leave of absence in 1933. Hunt was also transferred to the English Department where for a short time he taught the public speaking course during one term and a course in the history of criticism during the second.

But Hunt continued to coach the debate team. One of his debaters, Clark Kerr (class of 1932) and later President of the University of California, remembered Hunt with great fondness. He described him as a "unique person at a unique time in a unique place." He said he admired Hunt for his personal concern for students not only while they were students but for their entire lives. He credited Hunt, along with others at Swarthmore, for instilling in him the ideal that it was their purpose to contribute productive service to their communities just as the Swarthmore community had served them during their college days.[30] About Hunt's "coaching" of the debate team, Kerr remembered what other students of Hunt remembered: he gave no instruction about how to debate. Instead, he gathered debaters together and gave a few suggestions and then periodically directed them along their ways. Kerr described Hunt as one "who guided" rather than taught.

Kerr did not find debating contests challenging. He thought they were more contests of how well one could live up to the rules of academic debating rather than intellectual arguments about public issues. One innovation, however, provided a challenging exception. Kerr could not remember who initiated the idea, but someone (and he thought it might have been Hunt) decided that it would be intellectually demanding to have one of the Honors students publicly debate a well-known person on a pertinent public issue. In 1932 Kerr was chosen for this event and his opponent was Norman Thomas, then running for President of the United States on the Socialist ticket. Of course, the general question to be debated was whether socialism was a viable political alternative to the two-party system and whether socialism could address the pressing problems facing the country. With the help of other students and the faculty, Kerr prepared for weeks for this public debate. He later called it one of the most challenging and exciting experiences in his college career.[31]

But as challenging as this event may have been for Kerr, Everett Hunt was growing frustrated with his position at Swarthmore. He seemed in limbo. His department had been abolished. He had given up on his doctorate. He was not certain about what his actual position within the English department was since he and his one course in public speaking had only been added to the traditional offerings of the department. He was not even sure, given this change in departments, what his rank was anymore.

Beginning in 1927 he began spending some of his summers teaching at the University of Colorado in Boulder. Apparently, he originally went to Colorado to take courses. In a letter to Robert Spiller, he briefly described the university and his satisfaction with the course in German he was taking in hopes of "getting on with my course in Kant next fall."[32] (Whether he was talking about a course he was to teach or one he was to take at Columbia is unclear.) But the letter is mostly about trips into the mountains which he fell in love with ("I walked sixteen miles yesterday"), and his ambition to climb Long's Peak.

For a number of summers thereafter he and Dorothy would journey to Boulder. One reason for this was that Swarthmore did not conduct classes during the summer and he needed to make additional money. Another was that it gave him an opportunity to teach rhetoric once again. A final reason was that Dorothy longed for the West. His son Alan (who was born in that fateful year of 1929 and must have been one very bright spot in that otherwise dreary year) explained that it was "hard for her to live, as she put it, 'in a hollow' in Swarthmore, Pennsylvania, a place where she said you couldn't see much sky even if you got up on a hill. What saved her from what might have been serious melancholy—not a natural condition for her—were the long (academic) summers spent in Colorado and Wyoming during most of the last twenty years of her life."[33] In Colorado Everett climbed mountains and rode horseback, two avocations he greatly enjoyed. Less athletic than her husband, Dorothy accompanied him on his mountain-climbing stints, but usually by car.

At Colorado he was welcomed into the university. Certainly, the fact that George Norlin, the great translator of the works of Isocrates, was president of the University helped make Everett feel even more at home. They met also Dayton McKean and Franklin (Dank) Folsom, recent graduates of the University of Colorado, who were to become life-long friends. McKean went on to Princeton, became a distinguished political scientist, administrator and author. Folsom was a bit different. At the time of his graduation he had read "everything that had been written by or about hoboes . . . and planned to take to the road after graduation, but these high hopes had to be postponed. A Swarthmore English professor [Everett Hunt], in Boulder for the summer, found himself unexpectedly without an instructor in his department [and finding] that I had no respectable job plans . . . he provided me with some."[34] Folsom spent two years at Swarthmore (1928-1930) before gaining a Rhodes scholarship. He spent much of his career championing leftist causes and writing books for adults and children. They exchanged visits in the East and the West and maintained a correspondence until Hunt's death.

At about the same time Hunt began to cast about for other teaching opportunities. During one of these visits to another campus, he ran into President Aydelotte. As Hunt recounted this meeting, Aydelotte was startled to see him there and asked what he was doing.

"Looking for another job," Everett replied.

"Why?"

"Because you abolished my department, and I don't even know what my rank is."

Aydelotte assured him that he wanted him to remain at Swarthmore and that his rank as full Professor would be transferred to his new department. He asked Everett what interested him other than public speaking and rhetoric. Hunt told him he had always had an interest in the English metaphysical poets. Aydelotte suggested that he take a paid leave of absence to study them and come back as a professor in the English department. Being an Anglophile, he further recommended that Hunt go to a British rather than an American university. Hunt agreed, and so it was arranged and put in writing once Aydelotte returned to Swarthmore. In later years, Hunt chuckled over the changes in academic administration that now would never allow a college president to act as arbitrarily as Aydelotte had in those more innocent days.

Hunt's leave was scheduled for the school year 1932-1933, but it had to be postponed for a year when Alan Valentine, Dean of Men, resigned to go to Yale as Master of Pierson, one of its new colleges. According to Hunt, students petitioned Aydelotte to name him as Acting Dean of Men, and Hunt accepted on the condition that it be only a one year appointment.

The year he served as Acting Dean was a critical one in Swarthmore's history. The Depression had profound effects upon students, their parents, and the college. In his *Annual Report* for 1931-1932 President Aydelotte acknowledged a loss of $ 30,000 in income from the shrinkage in resident students.[35] The resourceful comptroller of the College, Nicholas O. Pittenger, made financial arrangements directly with students and managed during even these darkest years not to dismiss "a student from college for purely financial reasons."[36]

However, the costs of attending Swarthmore seemed prohibitive to prospective students. The faculty reacted with remarkable altruism. They voted to contribute a percentage of their salaries to a scholarship fund for students entering in 1933-1934. Those entering young men and women were forever grateful, and especially to Hunt who interviewed the men for admission that year and helped arrange for financial aid. In appreciation the Class of 1937 donated $ 33,000 for an endowed scholarship in honor of Everett Hunt in 1973. Others who attended Swarthmore during those Depression years felt equally indebted. Eugene M. Lang (Class of 1938) donated one million dollars for a music building. The Eugene M. and Theresa

Lang Music Building, a modernistic structure that has won several architectural awards, was the first building in Swarthmore's history to be specifically dedicated to the arts.[37] One room is named the Dorothy Rossman Hunt music room and houses her grand piano, donated after her death.

Such was the effect of Hunt's first foray into administration. When he returned from Europe he would find that the one year's service would be extended into a new kind of human adventure that was to change his career and his life.

Studies Abroad

Going abroad was a new educational opportunity. Hunt had never studied abroad, had not been part of the British tradition. The tradition he chose, in turn, had few if any representatives in America in his day. He and his family first went to the ancient University of Edinburgh to study for a term with Sir Herbert J.C. Grierson, Regius Professor of Rhetoric and Belles Lettres from 1915-1935. Grierson was at the height of his fame. His investigations into literature of the seventeenth century had been instrumental in gaining modern recognition for John Donne, and had established new dimensions in literary scholarship. He was described as "one of the greatest scholars of the age of learning, to letters, and to the cause of university education."[38] Furthermore, Grierson had sympathy for rhetoric. His lectures on rhetoric, *Rhetoric and English Composition*, were eventually published during his retirement and revealed more of an inclination toward the Aristotelian conception of rhetoric than the belletristic tradition of his predecessors and successors.[39] About Grierson, Hunt wrote: "I went to Edinburgh [U]niversity to study John Donne and 17th century poetry with Herbert Grierson. I did this partly because I was told that I could come back and teach 17th century lit[erature]. Grierson was the man who really brought Donne back to recognition. I always enjoyed his many cracks at American Germanized scholarship."[40]

But the choice to study Donne and the other metaphysical poets was neither capricious nor dictated by professional interests. It was a personal choice. He was drawn to Donne and later to Milton as well, because these two poets of the sixteenth and seventeenth centuries reflected religious temperaments and orientations Hunt shared. In addition, that period of time seemed comparable to the early twentieth century: "It seems possible . . . that the disruption of traditional values, cosmological and political, which was occurring at the beginning of the seventeenth century encouraged this cast of mind [the love of paradoxes, the turn to a critical and speculative rationalism tempered by elements of mysticism] and that metaphysical poetry is the reflection of a peculiar tension between faith and skepticism."[41] Of course, T.S. Eliot had already helped renew critical attention for the metaphysical poets and had drawn a similar connection between their times and the early twentieth century, between their poetic responses and what were to become his own.[42]

But Hunt's interest was different from Eliot's, as different as Hunt's Quaker beliefs were from Eliot's despair and later conversion to Catholicism. He rejected the role of proselyter or disciple. In the chapter on the "divine poetry" of Donne in Helen C. White's *The Metaphysical Poets* Hunt underlined the following words: "The center of interest [in Donne's divine poems] is the devotee, not the Divinity. And it is the devotee in the singular person. The corporate 'we' of the preacher and the hymn-writer plays little part in these poems even as a rhetorical device, and practically none as a psychological fact. It is not the priest who speaks here but the individual soul."[43] Such sentiments accorded with Hunt's Quaker beliefs. However, I do not mean to suggest that these were the sole reasons for his interests in Donne nor that he was interested only in the metaphysical poets (though certainly their interests coincided with his own in many respects). Later, he would teach both the prose and poetical works of Milton whose style and substance would be quite different.

But choosing Donne originally and later moving on to other religious poets of the period was a choice dictated by Hunt's own religious concerns. Hunt was profoundly religious, but his instincts and beliefs were not sanctimonious, not doctrinaire. He was a man of religious piety, in the best sense of the word. He was devoted loyally to his faith as an act of the heart and he expressed his devotion through his reverence and respect for others. His Quaker faith and his rhetorical training bolstered his natural detachment, a stance that allowed him to be both critical and sympathetic. Late in his life he said to me: "I spent the first part of my life seeking to locate the place of rhetoric in the modern world and then to make that place humanistic. I spent much of the last part trying to discover the place of religion in the modern world, trying to discover its function, and trying to reconcile it with modern problems." I can only speculate, since Everett did not talk much about his teaching of literature, that he hit upon studying Donne and Milton because they represented attempts to place religion in their own worlds and adapt it to the particular circumstances and the intellectual as well as religious problems they confronted. But that is only speculation on my part. Suffice it to say that he immersed himself in the literature of the seventeenth century with special emphasis on the religious dimensions of that literature.

From Edinburgh Hunt and his family went to Oxford where one of his former students, Richard Kain (author of *Fabulous Voyager: James Joyce's Ulysses*), visited with them and later recalled Alan reciting "In the days of swords and periwigs" for their entertainment.[44] From Oxford they crossed the Irish Sea to Dublin and to Trinity.

Hunt rarely said much about what exactly he studied or learned while he was abroad. The notebooks he kept at the time are not very revealing either. He seemed to have used them to write summaries of and quotations from books and articles he read. For example, a typical entry is entitled: "Pater's Essay on Wordsworth" which includes his summary of the ideas of that essay. Another is "Latter Day Pagans, Symonds & Pater, *Quarterly Rev.*, Vol. 182, 1895."[45] There are also synopses of essays on American writers among them Hawthorne and Emerson.

What he did love to recall were personal experiences. "I took many climbing trips out from [Edinburgh] with a Scottish mountaineering society. And I shall always remember a meeting of the Royal Scottish Drama Society where I heard Bernard Shaw denounce them for asking playwrights to cut down on their royalties so that small Scottish villages could afford to produce contemporary plays, such as Shaw['s]. He was gayly [*sic*] sarcastic about the playwright['s] necessity for earning a living."[46]

When I was preparing to spend several months in Ireland and wrote Everett about the impending trip, he responded with a reminiscence of his days in Dublin: "I am glad to know of your interest in Ireland. My wife Dorothy and I lived in Ireland for a semester while I studied at Trinity College. We lived with relatives who drove us about on week ends if we would but buy the gas. We lived next door to the Yeats sisters, and I met WB [William Butler Yeats] several times at the Abbey Theatre. One of my students in criticism has become an authority on Joyce [Richard Kain]. I follow Irish news with deep regret."[47]

Only two years before he died, he received a delightful reminder of his days in Ireland: "Lester Thonssen writes me from Denver that he recently attended a cocktail party at which a touring Irish family asked him if he ever knew Everett Hunt. The Irish lady told him that her parents had entertained me and my wife Dorothy and son Alan when I was studying in Dublin, and had driven me all over Ireland, and she, who was about twelve then remembered it all, and wanted to hear from me. I wrote her and have a long fond letter from Belfast."[48] Such were the warm human relations and memories of Ireland.

At year's end, he returned to Swarthmore to take up his new duties as Professor of English and to embark upon a new career.

Professor of English Literature

When the Hunts returned to Swarthmore, they moved into 604 Elm Avenue which they rented from the College, and he would remain there until his retirement in 1959. His first teaching duties were courses in "Spenser and Milton" (which was changed in 1936 to "Milton and the 17th Century" and concentrated on poetry of the Old Testament, John Donne, and Milton) and in "Criticism" ("Classical background of English Criticism in Plato, Aristotle, Longinus and Horace, representative essays of major English Critics from Philip Sidney to Walter Pater, brief survey of problems and writers of contemporary criticism.") He also team-taught an Honors course (a half-course it was called) in "Victorian Literature and American Literature" with Robert E. Spiller.

Robert E. Spiller was the one of the founders of American Studies. His first book, *The American in England During the First Half Century of Independence* (1926) had brought him immediate acclaim, and the many books that followed confirmed that the acclaim was not misplaced. In paying tribute to him in 1978, Hunt quoted from a tribute given five years before: "Dr. Spiller will be honored not only because he is America's most eminent literary historian, literary critic, and scholar, but also because of his founding of American Studies courses in numerous American, European, Indian and Asian countries."[49] When Spiller and his co-editors put together their three volumes of the *Literary History of the United States*, he prevailed upon Hunt to write the chapter on "The Orators." Even after Spiller left Swarthmore for the University of Pennsylvania, they remained friends and with their families, they occasionally vacationed together at the Colonial Hotel in Cape May.

Harold C. Goddard headed up the English Literature Department Hunt joined and served Swarthmore for 37 years. To academics outside of English profession, he is probably best known for his book, *The Meaning of Shakespeare* (1951). The book, Everett said, had world-wide influence, despite the fact that some critics said he wrote like a "pious orthodox Quaker." Hunt later reviewed the book warmly for both the *Phoenix* (the Swarthmore College newspaper) and the *Quarterly Journal of Speech*.[50] When Goddard retired in 1946 his students presented him with 58 published letters of tribute that showed, as Hunt noted, "what a teacher may mean to his students, personally, intellectually, and in the shaping of ideas." Hunt went on to describe Goddard as a teacher students regarded as a "saint."[51]

Everett now began teaching literature in the English department and teaching Milton as an honors course. It may be appropriate to describe briefly how reading for Honors worked at Swarthmore. At the end of their sophomore year, students were allowed to apply for Honors studies. If they were admitted, their last two years of studies differed greatly from their first two years of traditional courses. Honors students would elect to study several subjects within a broad field of interrelated subjects. For example, in 1926, the Division of English Literature was conducted jointly by the Departments of English, History, and Philosophy.[52] Classes for Honors were limited to five or six members. Students met for several hours in two weekly seminars, usually in the home of one of their instructors. Extensive reading lists were drawn up, and discussions of these readings as well as short papers were critical and lively. At the end of these final two years of intensive and extensive study, students submitted to be examined by external experts brought in by the College. Hoyt Hudson was one such examiner and described the rigor of both the written and oral examinations required of students.[53] The competition for admission to Honors was fierce, and the competition among Honors students was fiercer still. Such rigorous intellectual work helped create Swarthmore's reputation as an outstanding college, but it also contributed, as we shall see, to some of the psychological problems of adjustment for students, problems that Hunt would later address directly as Dean of the College.

One of the books Hunt used to teach his course on Milton was Frank Allen Patterson's edition of the complete poems, *The Student's Milton* (1930). In his copy of the book, I found several sets of review questions and final examination questions dated from 1938 to 1955. The questions show a strong rhetorical bent, more so than a literary one. There is an emphasis on the arguments presented in various readings and questions about the relationship of readings to problems of the modern world. A few examples should demonstrate this bent. The 1951 examination included: "Show how Milton was both a natural rebel and an upholder of authority." From the 1952 final examination: "What argument in the Areopagitica is of central importance in Paradise Lost?"; "State the arguments of Moloc, Belial, and Beelzebub, and show how they illustrate Milton's training in argument;" "Of three interpretations of Paradise Lost, Puritan, romantic, and humanist, select the one you think most important and state it as clearly as possible." A 1955 examination asked: "State the principal themes of the Prose Works of Milton that you have read, show their underlying unity, and state what significance they may have for the present." This particular exam had as its final question: "Write your own question and answer it."

But Hunt's enthusiasm for Honors work was tempered by his skepticism about placing too much emphasis on purely intellectual matters. He voiced his reservations in his address to the opening of honors work in 1935, an address that was printed in *School and Society*.[54] Contrasting Milton's early description of a full education and his high hopes for it with his later disillusionment with education, Hunt asked: "We have been educational reformers, and we have sometimes called the intellectual fare on which we were raised a feast of sow thistles and brambles; are we not inviting our students to make a similar response to our programs if we set up an ideal as impossible as Milton's? Or, if we do not merely depress our students, are we producing arrogant young intellectuals, fond of theory, contemptuous of their elders, lacking in judgment and devoid of common sense?" How to achieve balance between these extremes? That question was a typical question for Hunt, and he answered it in typical fashion, not by announcing a creed but by suggesting habits of mind and feeling that would lead students to make their own choices.

Hunt began with his conception of what a liberal education should do: create the liberal person for practical citizenship. To demonstrate what he meant he quoted a long section from Isocrates where that ancient Greek described wise people as those "who manage well the circumstances which they encounter day by day and who possess a judgment which is accurate in meeting occasions as they rise and rarely miss the expedient course of action . . . ." To achieve these purposes Isocrates recommended the qualities of decency and honor, an agreeable and good-naturedly attitude toward others, and an inner belief not to "desert their true selves." Hunt believed education ought to serve these purposes.

To achieve this practical wisdom, Hunt counselled that intellectual knowledge be combined with common sense which he defined as "the ability in any situation to make the best guess about what to do." Here Hunt was returning to his early arguments with Woolbert and O'Neill, to the early divisions he and they had made between a scientific (or strictly professional) search for certainty in intellectual matters and a rhetorical search for the best possible course of action in an uncertain world. But "guessing" was neither capricious nor uninformed. The kind of common sense Hunt had in mind was far more complex: "Common sense is common, not because everyone has it, but because a number of senses must work together in common to achieve a single result; they must be integrated according to the purposes of the individual, and they must work together in situation of varying degrees of complexity."

The warfare between expert knowledge and informed common sense, Hunt noted, had been central in the arguments between the Bacons and Huxleys, on the one hand, and the Arnolds and Butlers, on the other, for control of education. The former sought an education in the interests of creating the kind of knowledge that would produce scientists and experts; the latter sought an education based on disciplined taste that would produce genteel generalists. Although Hunt's sentiments clearly tipped toward Arnold and Butler, he said that both the sage and expert, "bold guessers and safe, kindly routiners" were needed and that the "struggle is not to prove one party right or wrong, but to achieve a balance in which each individual can realize his fullest growth." To grow required an environment of freedom. So, Hunt concluded his address by advising the student assembly to use their freedom wisely—making sound choices in work and play, in interests and activities, recognizing that all are part of the whole, each contributing its special value to the making of the complete person.

This brief summary cannot do justice to the grace and humaneness of Hunt's address, and the reader is directed to the full text as one of the best statements of his attitudes toward education. It contains familiar themes that he had voiced before, but these themes are adapted to the particular circumstances of Honors work at Swarthmore. The humanistic spirit animates the entire address. His defense of the traditional values of decency, honor, and magnanimity was balanced by his concern for the individual's personal growth. Above all, he exemplified that of which he spoke. Years later, it would be said of him: "We who have learned that in college one studies not courses but men remember Milton, yes, but Everett Hunt perhaps more."[55]

Literary Essays: 1932-1938

Now teaching in the English department Hunt sought to adapt to the professional responsibilities of a professor of literature. That meant attending academic conferences and writing and publishing essays on literary topics. But even as these topics were ostensibly literary, each had a strongly rhetorical perspective and in one way or another turned back to Hunt's rhetorical and humanistic concerns. Several of these command our attention at this time.

At a symposium in 1934 on "Literature and Society" at the College Conference on English in the Central Atlantic States, Hunt appeared with the Communist, Granville Hicks. Only the year before Hicks had published *The Great Tradition: An Interpretation of American Literature Since the Civil War* while he was very much under the spell of Marxism, so much so that he had joined the editorial staff of *New Masses*. In his address to the Conference, "Literature and Revolution," he defended the pathetic proletariat novels, arguing that they were in their infancy and needed time to mature. But his principal argument—the one that had brought him to prominence in the first place—was that writers must develop a class consciousness to produce significant social literature and that critics should adjust their standards to meet Marxian interpretations of society.[56]

In his address, "The Social Interpretation of Literature," Hunt wryly admitted that Hicks' doctrine had virtues. It "orders all our conflicts, divides our writers neatly into schools, explains all their failures, and fills us with a long unfelt glow . . . ."[57] But he replied to insist on "praising the strength and worth of the proletariat, to demand an optimistic faith in the revolution, is to compel authors to write by formula and to substitute rhetoric for art."[58] Writers would no longer be free to write as they wished, but would be confined to hymns of praise to Marxism. In addition, critics, were they to follow Hicks, would not judge literature on its own merits, but by the standard of a particular political or economic system. Such an economic doctrine as a basis for literary criticism was no worse, Hunt noted, than a theological or psychological one, but such criticism would necessarily ignore great works of literature or distort them to fit Marxist tenets.

Hunt did agree with Hicks on the need for studying literature to produce an imaginative realization of the world-view of great writers, rather than have criticism concentrate on the techniques of writing:

> Anyone who has gone through the controversy over Matthew Arnold's 'criticism of life' knows how inadequate that formula has been found. In the face of all that, I am willing to subscribe to it, for purposes of teaching at least. I hope teachers will always recognize the large element of enjoyment in literature, beyond all explaining or interpreting, and will to some extent leave students alone to enjoy. But so far as the intellectual processes of teaching are concerned, a discussion of the world-attitude of the author seems to me to be most truly liberal way of teaching.[59]

Unlike Hicks, Hunt proposed to study the varieties of "world-attitudes," created by writers instead of subordinating art to a particular political "world-attitude."

The thoughts of this essay were consistent with others that Hunt had presented. He agreed with Hicks that literary criticism should go beyond aesthetics and the technical problems of literature to criticize life. At the same time, he rejected ideology as the sole method for doing that because to accept such a position (as the one Hicks advocated) required one to become doctrinaire about one's own criticism. Such a position was far from Hunt's temperament. He was much too much the idiosyncratic humanist. Indeed, he was so much the humanist that he censured other humanists who would make humanism into a dogma. In reviewing Robert Shafer's *Paul Elmer More and American Criticism*, he expressed admiration for More, but reproved Shafer for making More's humanism into a method of salvation for society. He stated that "Mr. Shafer has treated Mr. More as some of our humanists always treat literature,—as a source of doctrine." He concluded that humanism needs to be "saved from its friends."[60] Such were the paradoxes of Hunt. He was, as he described Matthew Arnold, "a moralist among aesthetes and an aesthete among moralists."[?61] And it was to Arnold that he turned for the model of his own intellectual efforts.

In the mid-thirties Hunt published two essays on Arnold: "Matthew Arnold: The Critic as Rhetorician" (1934), and "Matthew Arnold and His Critics" (1936). In the first he sought to present Arnold's conception of criticism and in the second to note his critics and to defend Arnold against them.

Although Matthew Arnold condemned the rhetoric practiced in his time, he did so, Hunt believed, because it "lacked the tolerance and detachment and wisdom that come from a wide acquaintance with the best that has been said and thought."[62] Hunt pointed out that Arnold distinguished between "rhetoric," which he saw as flattery, and "persuasion," which he thought of as a method of expressing criticism. Arnold attacked the former while praising the latter. Thus, what he attacked was a certain constricted notion of rhetoric. What he practiced, as Hunt observed, was the Aristotelian conception of rhetoric. In actuality, Arnold's literary criticism was identical in function with Aristotelian rhetoric, especially when applied to subjects other than literary, because he intended to persuade the public and because he argued the topics

Aristotle assigned to rhetoric—ethics, politics, and the other general ideas upon which people are called to deliberate.

Arnold believed that the critic should examine literary ideas as a guide to conduct, as a criticism of life. To do so required that he persuade his reader that particular ideas are more desirable than others. Thus, Arnold enlarged the conception of literary criticism to encompass more than technical, aesthetic evaluations of creative works. In fact, his conception often had little to do with literature at all:

> It is criticism of all branches of knowledge—theology, philosophy, history, art, science, to use Arnold's list—if the tone and temper and method, and oftentimes the scale of values, are taken from literature. That is, literary criticism takes its meaning from its method and tone, not its subject matter.[63]

The methods and aims of Arnold's literary criticism coincided with Hunt's view of the function and methods of rhetoric. Both differ from scientific methods and specialized aims because both draw for sustenance upon the traditions of the best that people have thought as guides to understanding and criticizing the present. Furthermore, Arnold insisted that "the intuitive as opposed to the logical method of persuasion is best both for discovering and for teaching truth."[64] Those who committed themselves to such an approach would seek to develop a critical intelligence rather than a critical method, and that intelligence would find its primary source in intuition. These intuitions, though not rational in origin, "are not revelations, they do not come to the untrained and unlettered mind. They come from literary tact, the result of wide reading in the best books."[65] And to achieve that "literary tact" would require all the reading, thinking, feeling, and living one could absorb and bring to bear on the problems of society. Such an approach to criticism, Hunt observed, contrasted sharply in method and purpose from contemporary scholastic criticism written principally for other scholars for professional purposes. Arnold, as critic and thinker, defied simple classification, but Hunt concluded that "the intuitions of a disciplined spirit and the persuasion of an accomplished rhetorician will always have their place in criticism."[66]

The language Arnold used in the nineteenth century may more confuse than enlighten a twentieth century reader. So it may be useful at this point to clarify some of the principal concepts of this part of Arnold's thought and show how they related to Hunt's particular views. "Literary ideas" were not ideas embodied in creative literature, but rather were social, political, educational and philosophic ideas that *literati* contemplated, discussed, debated, and wrote about. They were the "general ideas" or persistent questions of culture and practical politics that Hunt had described. Arnold's "critic" was his description of the ideal person to address these questions. The critic, in Arnold's usage, was synonymous with the last century's designation of "man of letters" (to use the precise description in those sexist days), with the social critic of our times, and with Hunt's ideal rhetorician. The purpose of their intellectual activity was to range widely over these general ideas with learning and grace, to criticize life, and to provide guides for conduct and living.

In a lecture given twenty years later Hunt expanded the qualities that make up the general ideas, qualities that must be added to the intellectual ideas and that rhetoricians and critics must preserve. Drawing again upon Arnold, he said: "Ardor, love, self-renouncement, and aspiration are essential to an abundant life .... They are poetic qualities; their protection is the duty of the literary critic, as their creation has been in part the work of the literary artist."[67] To these responsibilities Hunt gave the following intellectual and poetic charge to contemporary rhetoricians:

> The critic as guardian of health-giving and animating emotions must protect them from the dangers of specialization, self-interest and all their works, whether they appear in scientific narrowness, dogmatism, enervating scepticism, false interpretation of literature, the confusion of means with ends, the flatteries of designing rhetoricians, or the routine of the practical life. As far as the critic is a specialist, he is so in receiving the ennobling experiences which the greatest spirits offer us in literature. In defense of the permanent possibility for mankind in

general he must 'get up' many cases in which he follows his authorities. His equipment is the judgment which is formed in the study of great literature, and which may be quite free from controversial workings or logical deductions. With this judgment, or intuitive perception, really, he defends literary truth from all fanatics, eccentrics, merely practical men, or undisciplined romantics.[68]

In his book, *The Rise and Fall of the Man of Letters: A Study of the Idiosyncratic and the Humane in Modern Literature*, John Gross remarked that until World War I such a person was a familiar part of the cultural landscape of society, only to be replaced after that by "academic experts, mass media pundits, cultural functionaries."[69] Hunt found in Arnold's critic and the "man of letters" a model for his own belief in the mission and function of the rhetorician in modern society. And to defend that conception required that he defend Matthew Arnold as well.

In "Matthew Arnold and His Critics," Hunt ventured to summarize many of the conflicts produced by Arnold's ideas and criticism. The main controversies concerned these assertions:

as a literary critic, Arnold too often abandoned literature; he trespassed flagrantly in the realms of theology, philosophy, and social science; his criticism was authoritarian and rationalistic; he commended poetry to his readers, not for its own sake, but as a guide of life, and thus he is inevitably a hopeless moralist.[70]

Hunt began his essay with a survey of each of these accusations, but in so doing, he was surveying the same accusations that had been hurled at him and his conception of the function and scope of rhetoric. Woolbert and O'Neill had accused him of leaving speech to trespass in other fields. In defending Arnold, Hunt was defending himself. The issues, whether they arise in literature or rhetoric, concern one fundamental question in criticism, "is the literary critic a technical analyst of literature, asking only, what does the author propose to do and how does he do it, or does the critic make use of his own values derived from all the living that he can encompass, and insist upon discussing any values that seem relevant.[71]

If the critic's duty is limited to that of technical specialist, then Arnold and Hunt were guilty of the charges leveled against them. However, Hunt argued that the questions Arnold asked admitted of no authority higher than the "continuous discussion of critical minds."[72] Neither specialists nor scientists nor ideologues nor even men like Arnold and Hunt could solve them. They were questions persistent in the history of ideas, persistent problems confronting practical public figures in every civilization. For example, Arnold and Huxley had debated the merits of an education based on literature versus an education based on science. Arnold claimed that literature could serve as a guide for conduct; Huxley made the same claim for science. Hunt observed that I.A. Richards and Max Eastman, among others, had revived this controversy. In 1962 Sir C.P. Snow and F.R. Leavis battled each other over the same problem.

Hunt concluded his study by noting that the issues that Arnold addressed had not yet been settled nor abandoned. They remain unsettled because they admit of no final answers, and each generation will produce its own critics (and intellectuals) who will produce their own truths and eventually will have "some small part of their judgments accepted as belonging to the wisdom of the ages."[73] These questions have not been abandoned because they contain essential queries about the quality of one's life, and what methods should guide one in deciding how one should live. Those were Hunt's central concerns, more than the specific or professional subjects of literature or rhetoric.

In Matthew Arnold, Hunt found a model and a defense for his own work. He sought in theory and practice a sound and unified conception of the function of rhetoric which would transcend routine technical studies and specialized scholarship, that would have a greater purpose than professional advancement or intellectual significance only to other scholars. Hunt, like Arnold, found this purpose in the study of the "best that has been said and thought." And each believed it his responsibility to pass on what they had learned in a spirit of sweetness and light. Just as Arnold would seek a method that would be useful as a criticism of life, so too Hunt wanted rhetoric to serve as a method to reach the same goal. Recalling

Isocrates, Hunt wrote that in the "disciplinary aspect of the attempt to be persuasive . . . one becomes virtuous."[74] Arnold's conception of criticism and his approach to it coincided with Hunt's conception of rhetoric and his approach, so much so that in writing his conclusion about Arnold he could well have been writing about himself:

> In his theory and practice Arnold offers a sound and unified conception of the function of criticism; he has made clear the realm of literary truth and the methods of working in it; he has exemplified a use of authority which mediates between dogmatism and anarchy, absolutism and scepticism; and he has shown that the discussion of significant ideas produces better criticism for the public than studio lectures on technique.[75]

So too had Hunt.

The essays on Arnold were Hunt's last forays into literary scholarship. During the last years of the decade his career would again change directions.

In 1938 Huron College conferred the honorary degree of Doctor of Letters upon Hunt and Hoyt Hudson. They cited Hunt for his "humanitarian work in education which has reflected distinction upon the profession of education, his alma mater, and upon himself . . . ." The frustration he had experienced in pursuing the doctorate was now assuaged by the honor his small undergraduate college had bestowed upon him.

At the same time Hunt had a flirtation with Stanford University. Stanford had been attempting to organize a school of the humanities that would unite languages and literature, speech and drama, the fine arts, history, philosophy, and religion into a unified school. Unofficially Hoyt Hudson had been working during summers with people at Stanford to create the new school. They wanted to hire him and Hunt, but Hudson originally turned down the offer because he believed that academic matters at Princeton required him to stay there, at least for the time being. Five years later, he would accept the Stanford offer.

Hunt's situation was quite different from Hudson's and he seriously considered the offer from Stanford. While he was in California for negotiations, he once again ran into President Aydelotte, this time in the Huntington Library. And once again Aydelotte was surprised that Everett was thinking of leaving Swarthmore. Upon learning this he reassured Hunt about how much he and the College needed him, offered him a raise, and promised to match the financial offer Stanford had made in a year or two. To give him time to make up his mind, he offered Hunt a leave of absence to try the job at Stanford and to consider whether he really wanted to move from Swarthmore or not.[76] Hunt decided to stay. Two months later Aydelotte increased Hunt's salary to $6,000 annually and named him as Acting Dean of Men. That salary was increased to $6,600 in 1939 and $7,000 in 1940. In addition, he was made Dean of Men and then Dean of the College in 1940, the same year that Aydelotte left for the Institute for Advanced Study at Princeton.[77]

At Swarthmore the position of Dean covered a multitude of activities; it was both an academic and a personal post. As Chair of the Committee on Men's Admissions his responsibilities included interviewing male applicants for Swarthmore both at the College and throughout the country, reviewing their academic and personal suitability for admission, and dealing directly with them throughout their four years at the College. Later this would also include counselling students about both their personal and academic lives. Hunt would extend his concern for students' welfare far beyond the four years they spent at Swarthmore, and that concern would develop into life-long friendships.

Perhaps, a story retold many times exemplifies how he handled his job:

> Irate parent, seeking son appears in Dean's Office. The Dean discovers son and pal have been in Florida for ten days. Parent (more irate) stamps on the floor. "You don't know a d—n thing about what goes on around this place, do you?"
>
> "No," said Dean Hunt, "I don't." The next development was a phone call from the Florida State Police who had traced to Swarthmore the license of an automobile abandoned on a Florida

highway. When the young men appeared, they were greeted by the Dean: "What are you going to do about that car you left on the road down in Florida?"

The boys observed, "You know *everything* that goes on around here, don't you?"[78]

In 1940 Hunt was given another "honorary degree," one that he prized just as highly as his Huron degree but one that would have a comical aspect to it. Out in Colorado again he climbed Mt. Lindbergh (later renamed as Lone Eagle Peak), a climb of over 13,000 feet that required rope work. To celebrate this feat his friends in the Colorado Mountaineering Recreation Faculty of the University of Colorado awarded him a "Doctor of Mountaineering" degree but added that it was awarded "without the knowledge or consent of the Board of Regents of the University of Colorado." Obviously, it was pleasant and harmless way of recognizing his climbing feat, and this light amusement gathered some publicity. Somehow the news story travelled as far as Chicago and attracted the attention of Robert Maynard Hutchins, President of the University of Chicago and *enfant terrible* of higher education, who publicly protested that the University of Colorado was giving academic credit for mountain climbing. Retelling the story later, Everett would invariably chuckle and remark upon the gullibility of intellectuals.

Dean Hunt, Swarthmore College

Return to Rhetoric

Dean Hunt's administrative duties were heavy and absorbing, but he did find time to write a series of occasional essays for the *Quarterly Journal of Speech* during the 1940s and 1950s. None were research articles, but rather were in the tradition of the nineteenth-century literary essays he had long admired and emulated.

In 1943 he wrote "The Rhetorical Mood of World War II," in which he reflected on the changes in styles between the rhetoric of the two World Wars. About the new war, he observed: "We do not hope fondly, nor pray fervently. We turn from words to things. Instead of teaching war aims, we teach mathematics and physics. And there is no proof that the boys do not fight just as well."[79] Such a change, he believed, grew out of a more sophisticated citizenry in which "people know too much about too many things" and therefore insist on combining knowledge with feeling in ways that had previously not been characteristic of a war rhetoric.

Two years later he wrote a moving eulogy of his long-time friend, Hoyt Hudson, who died unexpectedly at the early age of fifty-one. Of Hudson, he said:

> With inexhaustible fertility he was always casting out ideas for others to play and work with; he never had the least desire to pose as a savant or to exercise authority over his associates. His appearance attracted attention immediately—his fine head, his intense aliveness, the note of excited interest in his voice, and the gleam of humor ever ready to shine out with appreciation for the wit of his companion; but he never monologued, or attempted to dominate.

With such qualities he was at home wherever ideas were current; not a bohemian, he loved
bohemians, and had charity even for the pedantic drudge.[80]

Such words could only be written by one who had loved and admired another deeply. But his tribute
did not end with words alone. Hudson's fame was nation-wide both as a teacher and a scholar.[81] He had
published an edition of John Hoskins's *Directions for Speech and Style*, translations of Kant's *Religion
Within the Limits of Reason Alone* (with T.M. Greene) and Erasmus's *In Praise of Folly*, which had become
the Modern Library version of that classic, and a variety of other works. When he died, he left a number
of unfinished works. Hunt joined with others in seeing some of these to publication. In 1945 Grabhorn
Press published a limited edition of Hudson's poetry under the title, *Celebration*. That same year Stanford
published the completed first part of Hudson's projected two volumes that would have been his comprehensive consideration of liberal education. The part published was entitled *Educating Liberally*. Wilbur
Samuel Howell, Francis R. Johnson, and Hunt reviewed Hudson's partial manuscript on the epigram—three
finished chapters and part of a fourth which comprised about a quarter of what Hudson had projected for
the entire work—and recommended it for publication by Princeton University Press. It was published under
the title, *The Epigram in the English Renaissance* in 1947 with a Foreword by the three who cared enough
to see it through to publication.

In April, 1949 Hunt discussed the Harvard Report *General Education in a Free Society*, at the Eastern
Public Speaking Conference meeting and later published his remarks in the *Quarterly Journal of Speech*.
The Harvard Report was right up his alley. It proposed to establish a body of courses bound together by
the general knowledge and common objectives they believed students should possess. The purpose of this
introductory curriculum was to prepare students to participate fully in a democratic society. It made a
distinction between specialization and general education: "Special education instructs in what things can
be done and how to do them; general education, in what needs to be done, and to what ends."[82] These were
topics that had dominated Hunt's thinking since he first began writing in professional journals and had
remained the principal themes of his many and diverse essays over the years. As I say, it was right up his
alley.

In his address to the Conference, "Rhetoric and General Education," Hunt argued that general education
finds its ultimate goal in the creation of the liberal person, "the good man skilled in speaking."[83] He adopted
the recommendations of the Report and sought to place rhetoric at the center of the plan for general
education by making it the core that would hold together all the different subjects that comprise this kind
of education. Such a proposal by Hunt meant that courses in rhetoric and communication would not be
given separately but in connection with the courses in general education. They would lose their identity
as distinct disciplines to serve a higher purpose of integrating separate fields of knowledge. In this sense,
rhetorical studies would become studies in the humanizing synthesis of disparate specialties by concentrating on the themes that "present the greatest, most universal, most essential human preoccupations first."[84]

Harold F. Harding, editor of the *Quarterly Journal*, circulated Hunt's article among educational leaders
and teachers of speech for their comments which he published in a subsequent issue. The replies ranged
from Howard Mumford Jones' complaint, "What does Mr. Hunt mean by rhetoric?"[85] to Harold Dunkel's
enthusiasm for recognition of modern rhetoric's proper and significant place in the humanistic tradition.[86]
Teachers of speech were as widely divided. W. Norwood Brigance wrote that Hunt's proposal would lead
to the end of the teaching of speech. If technical training in speech was not separate from courses in general
education, Brigance warned that "after twenty years no genuine rhetoric would be taught in these courses,
and after forty years no semblance of rhetoric would be taught."[87] Edwin B. Pettet cordially embraced
Hunt's ideas. Teachers of rhetoric, he wrote, must educate the whole person, not the superficial person.
The "rhetorician must humanize his subject as *his* first duty. He must . . . become more than a specialist in
the techniques of rhetoric, its vocal problems, its audience analysis problems; he must become more than
an expert in semantics and in the use of words; he must become as at home in the pages of Aristotle as he
is in his speech text."[88] Hunt replied briefly to these criticisms and endorsements; he reiterated that he still
believed that rhetoric could be and should be a central study integrating various specialties with the

university into a coherent whole of knowledge. There was little more that he could say. He had heard all the criticisms before, long before, and his position remained as steadfast now as then.

Five years later at a professional convention program honoring Wayland M. Parrish of the University of Illinois upon his retirement, Hunt delivered his most succinct and eloquent statement about his conception of a humane rhetoric: "The case for rhetoric as a humane study may be stated with deceptive simplicity. Rhetoric is the study of men persuading men to make free choices."[89] But choices should not only be free, Hunt stated, they should also be enlightened:

> An enlightened choice is a choice based upon a wide knowledge of all the alternatives, but knowledge about the alternatives is not enough. There must be imagination to envisage all the possibilities, and sympathy to make some of the options appeal to the emotions and powers of the will. Such dignity as man may have is achieved by the exercise of free choice through the qualities of learning, imagination, and sympathy; and we should add to these qualities as a fitting accompaniment, what may be called civility.[90]

In this brief paragraph Hunt summarized his beliefs about his conception of rhetoric.

The key words for Hunt were: *probability*, *knowledge*, *imagination*, *sympathy*, and *civility*. Hunt did not believe that rhetoric was a specialized subject nor that it could be taught humanely through rules and techniques. He was concerned with the public and practical issues upon which all people are called to deliberate and decide, issues that resided in the realm of probability rather than in the arena of scientific or specialized knowledge. To decide these questions would require all the knowledge that one could gather. But even knowledge of the best that had been said and thought was not enough. Hunt was a man deeply in love with intellectual matters. But he also understood the limits of intellect and was critical of the claims of rational intellect to true knowledge or as a complete guide to conduct in life. Being intellectual meant that one was only a step away from being intellectually arrogant or dogmatic just as being a scholar meant that it was easy to slide into pedantry and specialized triviality. Thus to knowledge, he added imagination and sympathy as two preeminent qualities needed to temper, expand and humanize the intellect. He used imagination as Arnold had used intuition, a means for discovering the truths that intellect, dependent as it is on logic, cannot imagine. But the "truth" of which Hunt spoke was an individual truth, very much like the inner light of the Quakers, and even it had to be tempered by a sympathy for the inner lights and individual truths of others. Sympathy, as Hunt conceived of it, was not sentimental, but respectful, a knowledge of and feeling for the beliefs and emotions of others. To balance one's own convictions with a genuine sympathy for the convictions of others was to understand truly what Hunt meant by addressing ideas in the realm of probability. If such issues could not be decided decisively, then a humane rhetoric would be one that at the very least addressed them with civility. And it was to Isocrates once again that he turned for understanding that often misunderstood quality as well as for Hunt's particular perspective on rhetoric:

> Isocrates . . . defined the liberally educated man as one who, in an uncertain situation, could make the best guess as to what he ought to do next. Making these guesses upon the basis of whatever learning, imagination, and sympathy he could command, and strengthening all these qualifications by attempting to make himself and his conclusions acceptable to others, he might well acquire dignity and civility and become a persuasive man, a rhetorician, in the best ancient sense of that now debased word. He would become acquainted in a general way with those persistent questions about which generations of men continually debate, he would know the characteristics of different types of audiences, what kind of ends, aims, and values would appeal to them, and without necessarily attempting to be all things to all men, would both consciously and unconsciously attempt to commend himself as a personally trustworthy agent of the policy he was supporting.[91]

In these brief words, Hunt summarized forty years of thinking about rhetoric, its place in a democratic society and in education, and the qualities needed to cultivate and use it humanely. It was his personal credo stated with simple elegance. And it all came down to *ethos*, which Aristotle once wrote was probably the most potent force in persuasion.

Everett Hunt as Dean

Hunt's major influence at Swarthmore came as Dean from 1939 to 1956. He made the proper adjustments from the Aydelotte era to the next administration presided over by John Nason. Hunt noted the differences in their styles of leadership:

> Aydelotte had a flair for publicity and for attracting money in a time when money was not plentiful. He was a crusader for intellectual distinction, for the exceptionally gifted, and a fighter against mediocrity. He was confident and exuberant. "Damn the torpedoes," he could say, "go ahead." John Nason, too, wanted to go ahead, but he preferred to do some mine sweeping first. He took over when times were hard and were to get harder. He saw few sources of aid outside the community of those who knew and believed in the College. He had to seek areas of agreement to reconcile opposing forces, to be a good Quaker, and to harbor the Navy V 12 unit and the conscientious objectors at the same time. But ... he had brought the College through a World War and a subsequent inflation to a Republican victory, and has seen the national reputation of the College receive new tributes ....[92]

In addition to the financial and administrative problems, it was during Nason's administration that the College successfully integrated, absorbed the returning veterans into the undergraduate community, and made the transition from the hard 1930s to the affluent 1950s. In dealing with these transitions, Nason had able assistance, not the least of which was given by Everett Hunt.

It is not my purpose to chronicle Hunt's administrative work. Such a history belongs properly within a comprehensive history of Swarthmore College. Suffice it to say that he presided over men's admissions, advised students, administered discipline, and served as liaison between the student body and the administration and Board of Managers of the college. Such activities brought him into intimate contact with students and their problems as well as their aspirations. Over and over students and faculty commented on his unique personal touch and tact in handling the often delicate personal relations he encountered. Instead of reviewing these activities, it may better serve our purposes by noting certain avocations and extracurricular functions that engaged him during these years.

One of the additional duties of the Dean was to play the host to visiting lecturers and artists. In performing this service he was blessed to have had the enthusiastic support of his wife, Dorothy. He even remarked once that he thought the choice to name him Dean had been due more to his wife's influence as student and faculty hostess and figure in the community than to any particular qualifications he had. Such a modest statement about himself was typical of Everett, but it also contained more than a grain of truth. Dorothy Hunt was a lively hostess who, as her son remarked, delighted in the social as well as the artistic activities of the College community:

> Mother was equally a friend to members of the custodial staff at Swarthmore College, to faculty and administration and to the visiting lecturers and musicians it so often fell to her, as the wife of the Dean, to entertain. With at least one of these visiting performers—John Jacob Niles, writer and singer of folk songs, maker and player of dulcimers, and Kentucky gentleman—my parents maintained a lifelong friendship.[93]

Others who visited Swarthmore found in the Hunts a warm and gracious welcome. Sometimes such visits even had humorous sides to them. When Sir Wilfred Grenfell stayed overnight with the Hunts, he left his shoes outside his bedroom door in the European tradition. Everett dutifully took them downstairs, shined them, and returned them before morning. On another occasion, a visiting Englishwoman asked to be driven from a social event to the train she had to catch. Everett drove her and when she gave him a fifty cent tip, he respectfully thanked her and pocketed the coin.

For recreation Hunt bought a horse, "Sleepy," from Leon Saul which he kept at Ted and Esther Widing's farm in Newtown Square and which he rode throughout Delaware and Chester counties, often in the company of other faculty members, such as Helen North, who shared his love of riding. He was a familiar figure astride "Sleepy" so much so that hardly a tribute paid to him failed to describe him as a horseman.

Dorothy and Everett spent their summers at Teton Valley Ranch in Wyoming from 1943 to 1950. This came about during one of Hunt's trips to Detroit to interview prospective students. While there he met Wendell Wilson who owned a ranch-camp, Wilson bemoaned the fact that all of his young counsellors were being drafted. Hunt promptly volunteered to work for him. For the next eight summers, Everett served as senior counsellor for the boy and girl campers, and with Dorothy as accompanist, he often sang at evening entertainments. It was an ideal arrangement. Wilson was proud to have a prominent professor on his staff, and the Hunts relished the opportunity to return to the West without academic responsibilities. Alan Hunt noted that his father's true, if unacknowledged, responsibility at the ranch was to keep the cook and chief wrangler from killing one another on long pack trips.[94]

Their chief avocation, however, remained music.[94] They had met through music. Both loved all kinds of music. And music was one of the special bonds between them. Mrs. Hunt gave piano lessons, mostly to children, and taught music at the School in Rose Valley. She was herself a solo performer and skilled accompanist. They were active members of the Swarthmore Music Club and together they presented a wide variety of songs, Shakespearean to Lieder to Rogers and Hammerstein.[95] Once a month on Sundays they journeyed to Merion (a suburb of Philadelphia) to attend the "singing parties" given by Henry and Sophie Drinker. These parties were quite the event. Drinker had built his house around a music room that easily held two grand pianos, a Hammond organ, a string orchestra of eight or ten musicians, and seating for one hundred and fifty people on folding chairs. Drinker picked the music and conducted. All those who came had to be able to "sight read" music. The orchestra arrived at 3 p.m., the singing began at 5:30 and lasted until 9:30 with supper for all in the middle.[96] In addition to participating in such soirees, the Hunts led a full life attending to academic duties, gracing social functions, and sharing each other's company at concerts, lectures, and plays in Swarthmore and Philadelphia, often escorted to the plays by Jack Powell as their host.

Dorothy Hunt died in 1953. The Memorial Service, at her request, was at the Friends Meeting House, but without speaking. Instead Brahms German Requiem was played.

His wife's death deeply affected Everett, as one would expect. In a brief piece, "This I Believe" written at the request of Edward R. Murrow for a book by that title, Hunt wrote:

> This complex miracle of attitude and temperament seems almost to defy analysis, but we all know and recognize . . . these good soldiers. I have myself lived with one for more than thirty years, and now that she is gone I wonder more than ever at her courage with gayety and grace, her interest in and concern for others, her ceaseless delight in the daily pleasures of living coupled with her sympathy for all the ills that flesh is heir to. In all this she preserved a kindly tolerance for my lame and slow philosophizing, and recognized that some people are just that way. Had I gone first, I know that her grief would have been as great, but she would have faced the situation with a calm assumption that it must be met, and would have continued to be a source of strength to all about her.[97]

It was with "a calm assumption that it must be met" that Everett turned away from his personal grief to the agonizing problems of others.

In his final years as Dean, Hunt became increasingly concerned about the psychological problems that Swarthmore students encountered and about which he had to counsel them. He was particularly concerned that the intellectual rigor and pressures of Swarthmore had caused students to neglect the emotional and playful side of their lives. In a reverse of Woodrow Wilson's famous statement about the colleges of his time, Hunt now believed that the main circus was swallowing up the side shows to the detriment of the mental health of students. In 1952 the National Association of Student Personnel Administrators held its annual meeting devoted to the theme: "How Can We Effectively Develop a Sense of Higher Standards of Personal Integrity and Individual Responsibility in the University and College Community?" Much of one half-day session and parts of others were devoted to exchanging information about mutual problems that deans and psychiatrists encountered in attempting to improve the environment of higher education and in advising students who experienced problems.[98] As one invited to speak, Hunt presented his ideas in an address entitled "The Dean and the Psychiatrist." After recounting the development of the office of Dean in colleges and universities as an academic and administrative office, Hunt observed that student counselling now had become an additional responsibility, although the procedures and psychological methods for helping students still remained ill-defined and only primitively developed.[99] He noted that Swarthmore had begun to address the problem by hiring two psychiatric consultants, Dr. Leon Saul and Dr. John Lyons. For two years they had conducted a one-hour non-credit course attempting to learn from students what seem to be their central problems. Swarthmore had pioneered in treating students as adults. Now it would pioneer in treating their problems as well.

But Hunt went beyond merely reporting on what Swarthmore was doing. He acted as well. He successfully applied to the W.T. Grant Foundation for financial support for an experimental course over a three year period beginning in 1957. He enlisted Dr. Leon Saul, author of *Emotional Maturity* and *The Bases of Human Behavior*, and Professor Solomon Asch, well-known social psychologist and author of *Social Psychology*, to team-teach the course with him. The seminar met in Hunt's home and centered on the problems of emotional life that occur frequently in the process of growing to maturity:

> A central theme unifies the numerous problems that are discussed: the obstacles that arise in the striving to reach emotional maturity, and the ways in which they might be overcome. The issues under discussion, although they inevitably concern themselves with the difficulties of emotional growth, are by no means restricted to the abnormal. Quite the contrary: they have to do as a rule with problems that most persons encounter—the persistence of childhood patterns into adult life, the clashes produced by the needs for independence and dependence, the consequences of overindulgent affection, or of deprivation of affection in early years, sexuality and mating, the sources of the sense of inferiority, of compulsive competitiveness and hostility . . . .[100]

The seminar became a prototype for establishing and institutionalizing counselling services for students that went beyond academic or career counselling to address the emotional problems students encountered in that special transition from adolescence to the beginning of adulthood that we call the college years.

As Hunt listened to students and interviewed, he began to organize these materials. The idea for *The Revolt of the College Intellectual* originated from this course, and took shape gradually. Upon retirement he began to talk his material into a tape recorder which eventually became the book. As it developed it offered him the opportunity to consider changes among students as he had observed them through forty-three years, from the days of social parties to a struggling awareness of social problems, from the fad of swallowing goldfish to participation in demonstrations. The book charted these and other changes as they occurred at Swarthmore.

Hunt's principal concern was that students had become so intent on developing their minds that they had neglected to develop their emotional lives sufficiently to cope with the stresses and strains of adulthood. As Dean he had seen the results of this imbalance and had sought to minister to it, first, through personal counselling, then, through the experimental course, and finally, through recording his reflections and thoughts on the changing problems students encountered. The themes of the book were familiar ones: the limits of rational intellect and the need for a balanced and whole personality. Writing some years later in his book, *Puritan Boston and Quaker Philadelphia*, E. Digby Baltzell concluded:

Aydelotte was determined to place the Oxford stamp of intellectual elitism, as he understood it, on American education. He introduced the famous honors program at Swarthmore, deemphasized sports, fraternities, sororities (abolished in 1934), and the powerful men's secret society, Book and Key (modeled on Yale's Skull and Bones) . . . .

By the 1960s Swarthmore had become a highly intellectual but lonely and anomic campus. In his policy of intellectual elitism, Aydelotte had unwittingly atomized the student body, a process described by Everett Lee Hunt in *The Revolt of the College Intellectual*. The book was not widely read, yet it is a brilliant and perceptive predictor of the anomie and student unrest that marked elite campuses all over America in the 1960s. Hunt, who had spent his career at Swarthmore and was dean of men for many years, takes the reader step by unsensational step through the Aydelotte reform years and shows their atomizing consequences. What Aydelotte, though not Hunt, failed to see was that his elitism at Swarthmore was individualistic and antinomian whereas that of Oxford was intellectual within a context of strong class cohesion.[101]

In one sense, one might justly say that Hunt's early rhetorical training and his attempt to fuse intellect, sympathy and imagination into a humane study had prepared him well for his responsibilities as Dean and the progressive measures he took to adapt to the changing mores and problems of students. In the eyes of Swarthmore alumni Hunt's personal associations with students and his concern for their concerns were what they most remembered about him, were what they most revered about him. Aydelotte gave Swarthmore an intellect. Everett Hunt gave it a soul.

In 1956 Hunt had been at Swarthmore for thirty busy years. He had passed his sixty-fifth birthday; he retired from the administration as Dean Emeritus. The John Nason Award was presented to him, a handsome gift of $1,000 and a citation for "having made a distinctive contribution, beyond the scope of normal duty, to the life of the College community." Two years later the Pennsylvania Speech Association honored him as Speaker of the Year and gave him a plaque for "Distinction in the art of Speech used in the service of mankind." In 1959 a special panel was held in his honor at the national Speech Association convention at which time it was announced that Raymond F. Howes would edit a volume of essays by Cornellians in his honor. *Historical Studies of Rhetoric and Rhetoricians* appeared in 1962 published by the Cornell University Press. It contained Hunt's "Plato and Aristotle on Rhetoric and Rhetoricians" and "Matthew Arnold: The Critic as Rhetorician" along with the reprinting of twenty other essays, including such important works as Hoyt Hudson's "The Field of Rhetoric" and "Rhetoric and Poetry," Harding's "Quintilian's Witnesses," and an excerpt from Wichelns' "The Literary Criticism of Oratory." The dedication read: "To Everett Lee Hunt [:] a pioneer in the Cornell movement to revive classical rhetoric and the author of distinguished rhetorical studies . . . ."[102] It was fitting and appropriate.

But of all the honors bestowed on Hunt in his last years at Swarthmore, none touched him more than the one that accompanied the Nason Award. It is worth quoting at length:

Host, singer, dean, teacher, speaker, author, horseman and in all of these by deliberate design "amateur"—moved by Athenian reluctance to rule, by British disdain for the pompous, by the saddleleather friendliness of the Tetons, and by a universal love for all that is human—this is EVERETT HUNT . . . .

His deanship has been a gentle, witty, and wise improvisation, full of pipesmoke, understanding and a Quakerly gift for proceeding as the way opens. Opponent of the too frostily rational, his affectionate skepticism has shown a right way through personal trouble and institutional tangle not by abstract science but by knowledge of the occasion and the man, an Aristotelian knack for the proper hunch at the proper time. As dean, so also as teacher—no man of hard facts and regimented theories, but rather an issuer of invitations to the art of enjoying and of wondering, a person too well acquainted with human affairs to let them be over-simplified, too aware of their ultimate individuality to see them overgeneralized. He knows our human as well as scholarly frailties, and has doctored both of them with a similar prescription—one that combines perceptive listening, imaginative suggestion, and friendly, educated laughter. We who have learned that in college one studies not courses, but men remember Milton, yes, but Everett Hunt perhaps more.

And indeed Everett Hunt with Dorothy Hunt, host and hostess, members and friends of the College. The warmth of their presence has been like the warmth of their fireplace fire, generous and all-pervading, a catalyst of good conversation and mutual understanding. It has spoken in word and action, but also in music, a music that was and is Swarthmore music. Nothing of mechanism or deliberated effort stood between Dorothy's piano touch and music itself. Hymns, sonatas, cowboy songs, they picked us up and carried us with them, all the while expressing a sincerity and love of the genuine which our college music remembers and emulates . . . . Knowing you as we do, we now get braced "to see oursels as ithers see us [*sic*]." And like a bold message that once sang out from the water tower in painted letters across the old baseball field, we say "Good morning, Everett."[103]

Finishing his classes in May, 1959 Everett Hunt retired officially from Swarthmore College.

Notes

[1] Richard J. Walton, *Swarthmore College: An Informal History* (Swarthmore, PA: Swarthmore College, 1986), p. 3.

[2] *Ibid.*, p. 1.

[3] *Ibid.*, p. 7.

[4] Everett Lee Hunt, *The Revolt of the College Intellectual* (Chicago: Aldine, 1963.), p. 8.

[5] Walton, *Swarthmore College*, p. 25.

[6] Hunt, *The Revolt of the College Intellectual*, pp. xviii-ix.

[7] Walton, *Swarthmore College*, p. 36.

[8] Eliza Ulrich Ullman, "Swarthmore Chautauqua," *Swarthmore College Bulletin* (January 1975), pp. 20-23.

[9] "Notes on Hunt Family Genealogy," compiled by Everett Hunt in March, 1979.

[10] "Class of 1937 Honors Dean Hunt," *The Swarthmorean* (June 29, 1973), p. 1.

[11] Obituary, "Philip M. Hicks, Professor at Swarthmore," *Philadelphia Inquirer* (June 17, 1975), n.p.

[12] *Ibid.*

[13] Hunt, "Editorial," *Quarterly Journal of Speech Education, 13* (February 1927), pp. 50-51.

[14] Hunt, preface material to Wilmer E. Stevens, "A Rating Scale for Public Speakers," *Quarterly Journal of Speech, 14* (April 1928), p. 223.

[15] Paul Shorey, "Democracy and Scholarship," *School and Society* (December 24, 1927).

[16] Paul Shorey, "What Teachers of Speech May Learn from the Theory and Practice of the Greeks," *Quarterly Journal of Speech Education, 8* (April 1922), pp. 105-131.

[17] Quoted by Hunt in "From Rhetoric Deliver Us," editorial *Quarterly Journal of Speech, 14* (April 1928), pp. 261-262.

[18] *Ibid.*, p. 264.

[19] *Ibid.*, p. 263-264

[20] *Ibid.*, P. 264.

[21] *Ibid.*, p. 267.

[22] *Ibid.*

[23] *Ibid.*, p. 268.

[24] V.E. Simrell, "Mere Rhetoric," *Quarterly Journal of Speech, 9* (June 1928), pp. 359-374.

[25] Hunt, "The Fiftieth Reunion of the Class of 1928," unpublished speech ms.

[26] Letter from Hunt to Windt, April 5, 1968.

[27] *Ibid.*

[28] Hunt, "Frank Aydelotte," *Swarthmore College Bulletin, Alumni Issue* (February 1957), p. 31.

[29] *Swarthmore College Bulletin*, p. 35.

[30] Interview with Clark Kerr, November 20, 1989, San Francisco, California.

[31] All information about Kerr's debating activities comes from the November 20, 1989 interview.

[32] Letter from Hunt to Bob Spiller, July 8, 1927.

[33] Letter from Alan Hunt to Windt, November 29, 1989.

[34] "Franklin Folsom '28," in Franklin Folsom ,ed.,, *The Window Reopened* (Koenig Alumni Center, Boulder, Colorado: UCB Alumni Association, May 1978), p. 23-24.

[35] Frances Blanshard, *Frank Aydelotte of Swarthmore* (Middletown, CT: Wesleyan University Press, 1970), p. 256.

[36] *Ibid.*

[37] Walton, *Swarthmore College*, p. 94.

[38] Quoted from *Seventeenth Century Studies: Presented to Sir Herbert Grierson* in 1938, quoted by D. Ray Heisey, "H.J.C. Grierson—Modern Scottish Rhetorician," *Western Journal of Speech Communication*, *30* (Fall 1966), p. 248.

[39] *Ibid.*, pp. 248-251.

[40] Letter from Hunt to Windt, April 5, 1968.

[41] "Introduction," in W.H. Auden and Norman Holmes Pearson, eds., *Poets of the English Language: Elizabethan and Jacobean Poets: Marlowe to Marvell*, *2* (New York: Viking, 1950), p. xxxii.

[42] See the various essays in T.S. Eliot, *Selected Essays. 1917-1932* (New York: Harcourt, Brace and Company, 1932). I mention Eliot in this connection because Hunt had a first edition of Eliot's volume. The essays on "The Function of Criticism," "Thoughts after Lambeth," and "Second Thoughts about Humanism" are heavily underlined, the first with notes in the margins and at the end of the essay.

[43] Helen C. White, *The Metaphysical Poets: A Study in Religious Experience* (New York: Macmillan, 1936), pp. 123-124.

[44] Letter from Dick Kain to Hunt, October 21, 1983.

[45] Hunt notebook from the University of Edinburgh, untitled and unpaged.

[46] Letter from Hunt to Windt, January 27, 1974.

[47] Letter from Hunt to Windt, May 14, 1972.

[48] Letter from Hunt to Windt, September 1, 1982.

[49] *Ibid.*, quoted from the Bulletin of the Philadelphia Art Alliance, 1973. See also the tributes to Spiller in *American Quarterly*, *19* (Summer 1967), pp. 291-302.

[50] *Phoenix* (May 2, 1951), p. 4, and *Quarterly Journal of Speech*, *46* (October 1960), p. 332.

[51] Hunt, "The Fiftieth Class Reunion of the Class of 1928," p. 2.

[52] "Programs of Honors Work," Appendix in Robert C. Brooks, *Reading for Honors at Swarthmore* (New York: Oxford University Press, 1927), p. 137.

[53] Hoyt H. Hudson, "An External Examiner Looks at External Examinations," *An Adventure in Education: Swarthmore College under Frank Aydelotte by The Swarthmore College Faculty* (New York: Macmillan, 1942), pp. 125-135.

[54] Hunt, "Reading for Honors and Common Sense," *School and Society*, *42* (November 30, 1935), pp. 726-732.

[55] Typewritten statement with the following description by Hunt: "Written by Gilmore Stott for President Courtney Smith upon retirement from Deanship—Originally written for presentation of the Nason Award for distinguished service in 1957."

[56] Granville Hicks, "Literature and Revolution," *English Journal*, *24* (March 1935), pp. 219-239.

[57] Hunt, "The Social Interpretation of Literature," *English Journal*, *24* (March 1935), p. 214.

[58] *Ibid.*, p. 217.

[59] *Ibid.*

[60] Hunt, "Humanism and Dogma," review of Robert Shafer's Paul Elmer More and American Criticism, *Sewanee Review*, *43* (1935), p. 502.

[61] Hunt, "Matthew Arnold: The Critic as Rhetorician," in Raymond F. Howes , ed., *Historical Studies of Rhetoric and Rhetoricians* (Ithaca: Cornell University Press, 1962), p. 342.

[62] *Ibid.*, p. 343.

[63] *Ibid.*

[64] *Ibid.*, p. 333.

[65] *Ibid.*, p. 334.

[66] *Ibid.*, p. 344.

[67] Hunt, "Rhetoric and Literary Criticism," unpublished lecture at George Washington University, January 1958, p. 16.

[68] *Ibid.*, p. 17.

[69] John Gross, *The Rise and Fall of the Man of Letters: A Study of the Idiosyncratic and the Humane in Modern Literature* (New York: Macmillan, 1969), p. xiii. See also, Thomas Carlyle, "The Hero as Man of Letters: Johnson, Rousseau, Burns," Lecture V in *Heroes and Hero-Worship* (Boston: Houghton Mifflin, n.d.), pp. 215-271. This lecture written in 1840 was youthful and romantic but gives the flavor of the adulation Carlyle accorded to such a person.

[70] Hunt, "Matthew Arnold and His Critics," *Sewanee Review, 44* (October-December 1936), p. 449.

[71] *Ibid.*, p. 450.

[72] *Ibid.*, p. 451

[73] *Ibid.*, p. 467.

[74] *Hunt, "Matthew Arnold: The Critic as Rhetorician," p. 332.*

[75] Hunt, "Matthew Arnold and His Critics," p. 466.

[76] Letter from Aydelotte to Hunt, February 17, 1938.

[77] See letters from Aydelotte to Hunt, April 6, 1938; December 8, 1938; November 9, 1939; and April 3, 1940. In his 1939 letter Aydelotte insisted that Hunt continue as Dean as an attraction to whomever would consider being Aydelotte's successor at the College.

[78] *Swarthmore Phoenix* (December 13, 1955), p. 1

[79] Hunt, "The Rhetorical Mood of World War II," *Quarterly Journal of Speech, 29* (February 1943), p. 5.

[80] Hunt, "Hoyt Hopewell Hudson," *Quarterly Journal of Speech, 31* (October 1945), pp. 271-272.

[81] See John W. Dodds, Willis H. Johnson, and Hubert C. Heffner, "Memorial Resolution, Hoyt Hopewell Hudson, 1893-1944," Stanford University, 1944.

[82] Quoted by Hunt, "Rhetoric and General Education," *Quarterly Journal of Speech, 35* (October 1949), p. 276.

[83] *Ibid.*

[84] *Ibid.*, p. 278.

[85] "A Symposium on Rhetoric and General Education," *Quarterly Journal of Speech, 35* (December 1949), p. 421.

[86] *Ibid.*, p. 425.

[87] "Rhetoric and General Education: A Symposium Continued," *Quarterly Journal of Speech, 36* (February 1950), p. 5.

[88] *Ibid.*, p. 8.

[89] Hunt, "Rhetoric as a Human Study," *Quarterly Journal of Speech, 41* (April 1955), p. 114.

[90] *Ibid.*

[91] *Ibid.*, pp. 114-115.

[92] Hunt, "Nason at Swarthmore," *Swarthmore College Bulletin*, Alumni Issue (February 1953), p. 1.

[93] Letter from Alan Hunt to Windt, November 29, 1989.

[94] For a brief statement of his views on music in the academic setting, see his "Music in a Liberal Arts College," *Society for Music in a Liberal Arts College*, seventh annual meeting, Princeton University, published in its proceedings, 1956.

[95] *Ibid.*

[96] See Catherine Drinker Bowen, *Family Portrait* (Boston: Little Brown, 1970), pp. 175-181.

[97] Hunt, "This I Believe," unpublished 3 page manuscript. It was not included in Murrow's book.

[98] "The Dean and the Psychiatrist: A Symposium," *Mental Hygiene, 37* (April 1953), p. 177.

[99] Hunt, "The Dean and the Psychiatrist," *ibid.*, pp. 177-196. The paper was reprinted in the *American Association of University Professors Bulletin, 39* (Spring 1953), pp. 16-35.

[100] Hunt, "Thinking about Feeling," *Swarthmore College Bulletin* Alumni issue, (May 1958), p. 4.

[101] E. Digby Baltzell, *Puritan Boston and Quaker Philadelphia* (Boston: Beacon Press, 1979), pp. 512-513.

[102] "Dedication," in Raymond F. Howes (Ed.), *Historical Studies of Rhetoric and Rhetoricians* (Ithaca, NY: Cornell University Press, 1962).

[103] Xeroxed copy of statement issued from the Office of the President, undated, two pages.

5

Retirement

The week-end in May, 1959 when Everett Hunt officially retired from Swarthmore was a busy one. Not only did he retire, he also remarried that week-end on May 16. His new wife was Marjorie Watson. Marjorie's life had been devoted to music. She studied piano with Gertrude Wilde who had studied under Theodor Leschetizky in Vienna. An accomplished pianist as a child, she had become accompanist for Herbert Wilbur Greene, a distinguished teacher of singers, even while she was in her teens. Tired of being an accompanist to another teacher, she founded her own studio and began her career as a vocal teacher in Philadelphia. She maintained her teaching studio until May, 1988, even when it meant commuting from Swarthmore to Center City two and three times a week. She was the co-founder with James Montgomery of the Gilbert and Sullivan Players in Philadelphia, who performed all the operettas at one time or another.

Everett had met Marjorie years before when he and Dorothy participated in the Drinker's singing parties. As Marjorie told the story, Everett began to take singing lessons to make up for his loneliness after Dorothy's death. Soon, he was coming a little early for his lessons and leaving a little late. Their friendship matured over time into love and eventually led to marriage.

They decided to be married when Everett retired. Marjorie later explained that she had her own career and did not intend to be a faculty wife, even for the few final years Everett had left at Swarthmore. Together they bought the only home Everett ever owned, a stately house at 221 N. Princeton Avenue in Swarthmore and prepared to move Marjorie from her home in Germantown when they returned from their honeymoon.

But all did not go smoothly. Everett's lack of attention to details was a constant source of exasperation and humor in his family and among friends. Alan recalled that once his father had hired a mechanic to come to the house and repair his aging car. Doing as many mechanics do, he turned the car radio on while he was working. Hearing the music, Everett came out of the house to see where it was coming from. From the car radio, the mechanic explained.

"Imagine that," Everett said with some amazement. "A radio in the car."

His inattentiveness to detail did not fail him on his wedding day. As they were preparing to leave for the ceremony, someone asked Everett if he had the license.

"Oh, it was in a very safe place," he replied. It was locked away in a safe deposit box in his bank. Needless to say, there was a mad rush to find the bank manager and to convince him that the bank had to be opened on a week-end.

The wedding did proceed as planned, and the newly married couple went to the Poconos for their honeymoon. At the end of the first evening after walking to a hill to watch the sunset, Everett suddenly announced that they had to return to Swarthmore immediately. He had given his final exams but had forgotten to turn in the grades. And return they did to the final 25 years they would have together.

During the first few years of their marriage Hunt busied himself with talking about his experiences as Dean of Swarthmore into a tape recorder and then editing them into a publishable manuscript. First published in 1963, before the wave of confrontations, riots, and urgent rebellions crested in Europe and America, *The Revolt of the College Intellectual* spoke of a new type of college student: troubled, frustrated, gravely intellectual. In succeeding years it would seem prophetic. But at the time it gained little notice. After a second printing, it fell out of print, having sold only about 1500 copies.

Everett felt lonely on the days when his wife went to Philadelphia to teach her students. He eventually got around to suggesting that Marjorie's sister, Helen, come to live with them, and so it was arranged. The two sisters had lived together all those years before Everett had married Marjorie. Helen was an artist and became a different kind of companion for Everett. She accompanied him on his walks, delighted him with her paintings (of which he was always justly proud), and together the three of them formed a new and closely knit family.

During the first ten years of his retirement, Hunt was busier than ever writing, teaching religion and existentialism to local groups, attending professional conferences, and journeying to various schools as visiting professor.

Last Writings on Rhetoric

The various essays that Hunt published during these ten years were tied together by his persistent criticism of specialized research and his continuous plea to relate rhetoric to larger subjects so as to make such studies humanistic. These themes resonated throughout each of his speeches and essays. Each of his writings followed a familiar pattern, though it would be wrong to suggest that they were written by formula. Everett was too original for that. Instead, the pattern suggested his habitual way of thinking. He usually began with a statement of the current problem he was addressing, then related past writings on the subject to the present, went on to plead for more humane approaches to such studies, and concluded by recommending certain scholars whose writings exemplified concretely the kinds of work he admired. He wrote out each completely and fully—be they speeches or papers at conferences—with the particular audience in mind as well as the specific topic he was to address. And each was informed by the unique brand of humanism he had nurtured over the long years of reading and reflection.

His address at the twenty-fifth anniversary of the Pennsylvania Speech Association was typical of these writings. He accepted Professor Gordon Hostettler's invitation to address the convention in Pittsburgh on the subject of "Rhetoric and Politics."[1] Hunt began by surveying briefly the central connections between rhetoric and politics in the works of Plato, Aristotle, Cicero, St. Augustine, Machiavelli, Edmund Burke, and John Stuart Mill. The question he posed was whether the study of rhetoric and politics should be united with ethics and poetry to produce a breadth of appeal to layman and scholar alike or whether these subjects should be studied separately through minute analysis ("of marketing research and propaganda analysis") by academic specialists interested only in talking to other specialists? Anyone who knew anything of Hunt's thinking knew how he would answer his own question. The former he described as the humanistic approach; the latter as the beginning of a Third Sophistic. To illustrate the kinds of work that he imagined to be most ennobling and worthy he cited a variety of studies by scholars in history, politics, and rhetoric with special emphasis on Richard Hofstadter's recently published book, *Anti-Intellectualism in American Life*. His conclusion was vintage:

> The eminent names I have cited seem to agree that politics is a larger and more intellectual subject than rhetoric, but that politics cannot get along without rhetoric; also that effective rhetoric is the product of a broad liberal education, which includes examples of the best poetry and eloquence. Highly specialized studies are inevitable in our academic world, and they have their place, but they should be extensively supplemented by studies whose appeal, like that of rhetoric, is not limited to the specialist.[2]

Such were the thoughts of Hunt in his seventy-third year, thoughts little different from those he had expressed at the beginning of his career, but now adapted to a different subject at a different time to suit a different mood.

The following year, 1964, Hunt returned to Cornell as visiting professor to conduct a seminar in classical rhetoric. He used Wilson and Arnold's *Public Speaking as a Liberal Art* as his text, but his focus was once again on the function of rhetoric, not a philological analysis of it. That perspective was reflected in the topics for final papers he assigned:

1. Appraise President Kennedy's Inaugural Address for style and persuasiveness.
2. Using the Index to Peterson's volume of speeches, select three ideas which would be relevant for a speaker today, and indicate what audience and occasion would be suitable.
3. Reread Chap. 4 of Wilson's Text, and then apply the first exercise (p. 92) to the description of an audience for a commencement address at the University of Hawaii.
4. Summarize briefly the most important aspects of rhetorical theory developed by the Greeks and Romans (Wilson text, chapter 2) and make your own comment on what studies should be added because of the development of modern methods of communication.[3]

However, Hunt was invited to Cornell for additional purposes beyond teaching. At the time the administration was considering whether to continue, cut back or abolish the Department of Speech at Cornell. The issues were so tangled, mixing as they did academic imperatives with professional and personal politics, that to digress to discuss them here would serve no useful purpose other than to get bogged down in reliving old war stories. Everett did what he could to help save the department.[4] Over the next two years he wrote letters to the administration, enlisted support from alumni of the department, and gave encouragement to those trying to save the department. In addition to these behind-the-scenes activities, Hunt delivered a speech, "The Humanities and the Performing Arts," in which he sought to reconcile the performing arts with the humanities, the growing professionalism in teaching drama with the goals of a liberal education.[5] Read outside the context of the controversy at Cornell, it repeats Hunt's various ideas about the value of the fine arts within the tradition of liberal arts, much as he had always found music to have such value. Read within the context of that controversy it was Hunt's plea to the drama department at Cornell to join in supporting the continuation of the Department of Speech. These efforts were to no avail. Two years later the Department that Hunt, Hudson, Wichelns and others had brought to such prominence was abolished.

During the next three years from 1965 to 1968 Hunt journeyed to a variety of locations for speaking and teaching. Professor Ray Yeager and I invited him to give the key-note address, "General Specialists: Fifty Years Later," at the Bowling Green Conference on Rhetoric and the Modern World that first summer.[6] The following year he went to the University of Hawaii as Carnegie Scholar-in-Residence and Lecturer in Speech for the fall term. During that time he gave a short address on "Persuasion: Ancient and Modern" in which he predicted the increasing reliance on persuasion in world affairs, despite the ominous presence of nuclear weapons:

The world of tomorrow will be what it becomes because of the power of persuasion exercised by world leaders. The power of the bomb is not the most persuasive force in the world. The bomb brings its own limitations, and Russia and the United States fear to do anything which will bring the bombs of their opponents down upon them. They must learn to negotiate, to talk in terms of a common economic development and the welfare of the people, all the people of our one small world. It is the power of persuasion that must govern the world. And there is no leadership without speech.[7]

Professor Hunt after retirement from Swarthmore

He continued to discuss the relevance of Aristotelian rhetoric to the modern world of mass communication and concluded by saying that in the battle for public opinion if, "injustice is allowed to prevail, it is a reproach to the art of rhetoric. And so in the midst of propaganda full of false promises, of lying charges, of vilification of enemies we have to turn to counter-propaganda to expose it all."[8] The rhetoric he envisioned was a rhetoric that spoke to the concerns of people by addressing their common problems and enlisting their common abilities—their intellects, their sympathies, and their imaginations.

But his greatest delights in Hawaii were in swimming in the ocean, discovering the ethnic diversity of the islands, and his time as scholar-in-residence at Sinclair Library. His sole duty in that capacity was to sit in the Library for an hour each day and talk to whomever came to talk with him. He never ceased to be amazed that he would be paid for such a pleasant pastime. He wrote at the time: "My graduate seminar of 12 is hot on the trail of the New Rhetoric and is wondering if the English depts. will include it in their courses & take it away from speech. We argue . . . vigorously over Burke & Richards. But I should not be talking about shop at Christmas time. I love to hear the Hawaiians sing. They are relaxed & happy. I love going to the Buddhist Temple. And to the beach 3 times a week to swim. And to see what beautiful girls I have in my class, and how widely read & intellectually sophisticated they are."[9] Nonetheless by Christmas he had also grown restless and was ready to return home.

The following year I suggested to Professor Gordon Hostettler, Chair of the Department of Speech, that he invite Everett to be visiting professor at Colorado State University which he promptly did, and which Hunt promptly accepted. Everett was now 78 and I thought this might be a final visit to his beloved West. He spent the fall term in Fort Collins and was able to revisit some of his friends from the old days including Dank Folsom. But I was wrong about it being his last trip.

In the spring of 1969 Professor Bower Aly of the University of Oregon arranged for a full speaking tour for Hunt. Marjorie accompanied him, no doubt because they had been often separated during the last few years, but also in all probability because Everett had a fear of flying. Their first stop was the University of Missouri, from there on to the University of Washington and then to Oregon, and finally down the coast to San Francisco and Los Angeles. At each he delivered a guest lecture on "The Rhetoric of Violence," a most timely topic for those turbulent days.

In his address Hunt could not conceal his personal abhorrence of violence, his disdain for the attacks upon universities, and his social conservatism. Yet, instead of condemning such disruptions, as others had done and were doing, he recommended new studies of the "rhetoric of violence" and of the people who committed it. As he said in one of his sympathetic moments: "It [the revolts rocking the land] is a qualitative revolution on the part of the people who still find that something is missing in their lives, and they want to escape the limits of the material. They want an expansion of consciousness, a recognition of the unique value of the individual, roles in life that will never remain static, meaningful human relations in what they call participatory democracy."[10] He concluded:

> Some of us will hope that the outbreak of violence in recent years will be merely a passing phase in contemporary life. I'm afraid that it's likely to get worse before it gets better. [But] a study of its irrational demands, its misleading appeals, and I must admit, at times its very real victories for reform, will add to the power of a rational rhetoric as an instrument for social change through persuasive appeals for justice. And I hope we may make those appeals.[11]

A careful reading of his address reveals Hunt in his most prophetic mood. The religious impulse, rarely stated overtly but ever present, prompted him to see the violent discord he abhorred clearly and to attempt to salvage something of value out of it, something that could be ministered to and nurtured. Even as one says this, one must also note that Hunt, like so many others, exaggerated the violence that broke out during those troubled times, and therefore over-reacted to it, giving it much more significance than hindsight would accord it. No doubt this reaction was due to his respect for the orderly processes of change as well as his respect for social traditions. But it was also due to his belief, strongly held and often articulated, that persuasive rhetoric was the primary alternative to violence as a method for change, or as he stated another time, rhetoric was the last bulwark against violence and barbarism.

Hunt's final paper on rhetoric was delivered at the 1969 annual meeting of the Speech Communication Association in New York. His subject was "Lincoln's Rhetorical Triumph at Cooper Union," and he delivered his speech at the Union. That was a special thrill for him. He had long admired Lincoln from the days when he had required his students at Cornell to re-enact the Lincoln-Douglas debates to this opportunity to speak where Lincoln had once spoken. And his words matched the occasion. With his customary orderliness he deftly set the historic stage for Lincoln's speech and noted its most characteristic persuasive ideas and appeals. But his sustaining focus was what the speech revealed about the man, Lincoln, and about the qualities of practical leadership he demonstrated. Thus, Hunt concluded:

> This Cooper Union Address was persuasive in that it was the mature expression of the characteristic beliefs and reflections of a man of sound judgment, informed by historical research, and concerned with a choice between civic goods. It argued for a middle ground between extremists. It appealed to the intelligence and moral convictions of his listeners. It made an American tradition out of the startling contrast between his Western frontier appearance and speech on one hand, and his good manners, with the wisdom and common sense of his conclusions, on the other. Where can we find a better example of the Aristotelian faculty of discovering all the available means of persuasion in a given case? The Cooper Union Address was a rhetorical triumph in that it was perhaps an unprecedented combination of political skill with a nobility of purpose and lofty qualities of ethical persuasion, which are a permanent need of democratic society.[12]

Hunt's address was also a rhetorical triumph for him. It was the one sustained piece of rhetorical criticism of a speech he had written in his long career, and it provided a moving example of the kind of humanistic criticism he had long called for. His attention was on Lincoln's character as expressed in his address and on the prescient values that animated Lincoln's practical policies. He had repeatedly said that character is revealed by the ways in which one attempts to persuade others, and he found in Lincoln's address a model for the kind of practical persuasion and lofty politics that he admired. Scholarly specialists might complain that Hunt added nothing new to the academic study of Lincoln, but others could find in Hunt's presentation a persuasive appeal for the kind of qualities Lincoln exemplified both as a person, as a political leader, and as a speaker. What one concluded about Hunt's address depended on what one was looking for and what values one found important in criticism.

Lester Thonssen published Hunt's speech in *Representative American Speeches: 1969-1970* and introduced him as "one of the most distinguished members of the speech education profession. His keen insights and orderly analyses of the rhetorical art have greatly contributed to the establishment of speech as an intellectually respectable, humane discipline in the enterprise of learning. For over fifty years his name has been honored by all who respect the tradition of our subject and who see in it a proper and useful instrument for the disposition of human affairs in a democratic society."[13]

Hunt's final extended opportunity to present his views came in 1971 when Professor Ralph Towne of Temple University invited him to be part of a graduate seminar that would examine three different approaches to rhetoric and communication. Towne invited Everett to discuss rhetoric as a humanistic endeavor: "the point of view that guides such a man in the approach he takes, the questions he finds important, the methods he uses in his investigations."[14] Professor Thomas Scheidel of the University of Wisconsin had accepted the invitation to speak on the behaviorist approach to communication. As the third and final speaker, I was invited to discuss the perspective of the "radical humanist." As the class was set up, we were to come to Temple for three days on different weeks to meet with students for three hour sessions each day.

Hunt accepted the invitation, but as the time came near for the class, he grew increasingly apprehensive. He wanted to write a statement of his beliefs, but could not find the energy to do so, and that inability further increased his anxiety. Finally, he called Ralph to withdraw. The pressure of attempting to produce a sustained piece of writing had caused his angina to act up and he thought that at eighty-one he was too nervous to go through what he now saw as an ordeal. Ralph assured him that he did not have to write a formal paper of any sort and that the class periods could be shortened so as not to tire him too much. But still he resisted. Ralph then hit upon a solution.

"What if I invited Ted Windt over at the same time and the two of you could just talk together with the students?"

Everett thought that would be an imposition on me to come to Philadelphia twice, but if it could be arranged, he would be very happy to go through with the seminar.

Ralph quickly called me to explain the situation and to offer the invitation, and I just as quickly agreed to it.

Hunt's time in the seminar was a complete success. Once he overcame some initial nervousness, he charmed the students with the autobiographical bits of information about how he first became interested in rhetoric. He roamed over the debates with Woolbert and O'Neill with generosity toward his one-time opponents. He presented his views with conviction and answered their questions thoughtfully. But it was not so much his ideas that enchanted them as the genuine sincerity with which he presented them, not so much the reputation he had earned over the years as the humanistic qualities he embodied and exhibited. The Aristotelian notion of a positive and attractive *ethos* worked its magic in those few days and obscured or made irrelevant Everett's repeated apologies for being out of touch with current research or his claims not to understand much of contemporary scholarship.

As we were driving Everett back to Swarthmore after his last meeting, he asked if either of us had seen the rock musical "Jesus Christ Superstar." He said a friend had given him the album and he had found it very moving. He went on to talk not only about the music but also about the problems of relating the religious spirit to modern temperaments. Ralph and I shot glances at one another and exchanged smiles in our mutual recognition that Everett never ceased to surprise and amaze us.

The Final Years

In the last decade of his life Everett's attention turned more and more to religion. Perhaps that is a natural preoccupation as one ages, but I prefer to think that it was also a product of both his life-long religious impulses, his continuing curiosity about a person's destiny and the quality of one's life. During the late 1960s and early 1970s he taught courses in nearby Wallingford on the world's religions, on existentialism, and on the relevance of religion to the modern mind. He gave a series of speeches at the College on a variety of religious topics and wrote essays, several of which were published in the *Friends Journal*. Among the subjects he addressed were: "Quakers—Yesterday and Tomorrow;" "The Poetry of the Bible;" "Quakerism, Music and Worship;" "Job and William Blake on the Mystery of Human Suffering." In 1977 he deposited manuscripts of these and other speeches with the Friends Historical Library at Swarthmore.

He sent me several copies of two in particular, two that he especially liked or thought I would. One was written early in his retirement after President Johnson had given the 1964 Commencement Address at Swarthmore and had praised the Quakers for working for social justice long before others recognized that social injustices existed. In a speech for Collection (the student assembly at Swarthmore) entitled "The Quaker Faith in Speaking Truth to Power," Everett replied by surveying the uneasy relationship Quakers had historically had with political power and powers. He went on to examine four expressions of the "devil theory" in the rhetoric of Soviet-American relations, each of which he found wanting. His examination of the final "devil theory" typifies the approach he used in this address:

> Our final charge against the Communist devil is that the Communists accept violence as the essential means of social revolution, and we are therefore justified in regarding Communism as an absolute evil which must be destroyed. But the violence of our times cannot be laid exclusively at the door of the Communists. Neither the first nor the second world war was

spawned by Communism. The Russians are not responsible for the concept of blitzkrieg, or obliteration bombing, or for the first use of atomic weapons.

And so, when we come to weigh the real evils at the roots of our tragic conflicts, it is clearly obvious that they are evils that are all too prevalent among all mankind, and our Quakers are gaining increasing support for their feeling that we should not conduct our negotiations on foreign policy with an exalted attitude of self-righteousness.[15]

Hunt recommended that his audience read Senator Fulbright's book, *Old Myths and New Realities* as an antidote to the campaign rhetoric of that year, a bi-partisan campaign rhetoric that depended on "stereotyped labels," "narrow nationalism," and an "intensification of hate as a basis for our foreign relations." He recalled the Quaker leaders who had spoken truth to power "even when they [knew] that they had little chance of immediate success in their appeals." More such heroism, he said, was needed because "today penalty of failure falls on all men everywhere, and the Quakers [should be] eager to cooperate with all the rapidly increasing forces that really work for peace."[16]

The truth of which he spoke was not a universal truth, but the personal Quaker truth as illuminated by the inner light. And it was that inner light that had guided Hunt along his way through his professional controversies with others as well as his personal handling of students. If it was not always the "speaking of truth to power," it was the speaking of his truth as his inner light helped him determine it to people.

Some 13 years later he wrote "Wisdom Literature of the Old Testament" which I shall pass over quickly. In this short speech given at Friends Forum, he returned to the books of the Bible that he had taught in his course in seventeenth century literature: Proverbs, Job ("the incomparable masterpiece of the Bible"), Ecclesiastes ("the equivalent of *The Rubaiyat of Omar Khayyam* in our literature of wisdom") and Psalms. It was their combination of wisdom and poetry that he loved, and it was to them he returned again and again in his latter years. He found a serenity and spiritual solace in these books, and often his letters included some mention of one of them or a brief quotation.

In the last decade of his life Everett stayed close to home except for his annual vacation at the Colonial Hotel in Cape May. He would no longer travel to teach, even though occasional opportunities arose. As the years rolled by, he gave up driving and chopping wood for his fireplace. ("Our zero temperature," he wrote "with six inches of snow is milder than the weather my Colorado friends write me about, but it has increased our enthusiasm for our fireplace. I used to love the old saying that he that cuts his own wood is warmed twice, but I am now too old to do much cutting and am so grateful to my grandsons for bringing me car loads of wood and putting it on our side porch. They love to go to their farm up in the Pennsylvania Dutch country and cut down old trees. The wood they bring is well seasoned. Sitting by the fire on a snowy evening is certainly one of the greatest pleasures of life. I even turn to Whittier's much too long poem "Snowbound.")[17]

During those last years he began to gain the full recognition from his profession of speech and rhetoric that had previously eluded him. With a resurgence of interest in classic rhetoric led by Edward P.J. Corbett among professors of English and by James Murphy among professors of rhetoric, scholars began rediscovering Hunt's work. Of course, their attention fastened on "Plato and Aristotle on Rhetoric and Rhetoricians," and it was variously reprinted in anthologies, including Crocker and Carmack's *Readings in Rhetoric*, Aly and Aly's *A Rhetoric of Public Speaking*, and the section on the sophists appeared in Schwartz and Rycenga's *The Province of Rhetoric*.

In 1972 my little essay, "Everett Lee Hunt on Rhetoric" appeared in the *Speech Teacher*, and it seemed to draw attention to Everett's professional contributions. Several years later Helen North, Floyd Anderson, and Richard Enos among others organized a special panel at the annual meeting of the Eastern Communication Association in Hunt's honor. The three invited papers were given by Richard Enos, "The Eloquence of the Mute Stones: Implications of Greek Epigraphical Sources for the History of Rhetoric;" Ray F. McKerrow, "Richard Whately: Old Myths and New Realities;" and my own contribution, "Hoyt Hudson on Rhetoric." Professor North, Everett's close friend and colleague at Swarthmore, presided with grace and wit. Raymond F. Howes sent a copy of *Historical Studies of Rhetoric and Rhetoricians* that all those who attended signed to commemorate the occasion. But what Everett seemed to enjoy even more than the honor was the gathering of surviving old friends. Harry Caplan came in from Ithaca, Sam Howell from Princeton, John Wilson who had been at Cornell when Everett returned there fifteen years before, and many younger friends he had made in recent years.

That same year Governor Thornburgh of Pennsylvania issued a special commendation for Everett's eighty-ninth birthday:

> As Governor of Pennsylvania, I am taking this opportunity on behalf of your fellow citizens of the Commonwealth to send greeting on this, your eighty-ninth birthday. As Swarthmore professor, College Dean, foremost scholar in the rhetoric of Plato and Aristotle, and leader for half a century in the humane education of American thinkers in the arts of speaking and writing, I commend you.
>
> The Commonwealth of Pennsylvania is proud of your attainments. The nation is grateful for your benefactions. Thousands of Cornell and Swarthmore students remember your wise guidance. You have made Pennsylvania and indeed the world of scholarship more hospitable places in which to live and learn.
>
> Best wishes for a happy birthday![18]

Everett was not fooled. He knew I had worked as Thornburgh's speechwriter the year before. In a letter dated two days later he wrote: "I have just received a birthday greeting from Gov. Thornburgh. Only you could have written it, and your super-eloquent rhetoric out does anything in your Presidential course. How did you persuade him to sign and send it?"[19] Nonetheless, he was proud of it. He had it framed and had copies sent to Huron College, Swarthmore, and the Speech Communication Association, and each in turn printed the letter in one of their publications.

At Homecoming and for his ninetieth birthday Everett was a celebrated guest. Some two hundred gathered at Lang Music building to honor him on this occasion. Eugene Lang, who had donated the building, read from notes he had taken while a student in Everett's 8 A.M. literature class and fondly recalled personal anecdotes about his experiences with Hunt. Everett replied with reminiscences of his own. John McIntyre of the class of 1951 led the group in singing songs from the by-gone days, and Alan and Margot Hunt presented a cake with ninety candles with one more for good luck.[20]

A year later Richard Enos of Carnegie Mellon University and Otis Walter of the University of Pittsburgh organized a national symposium on Greek rhetoric in his honor. A number of scholars submitted papers and eventually seven were chosen for public presentation in the day-long meeting on March 21, 1981

The symposium also precipitated another anxiety attack. Enos and Walter invited Hunt to attend and present a statement. He misunderstood their request and thought they wanted a paper from him. After his experience with the Temple seminar, he no longer wanted to expend the energy to attempt any new rhetorical studies, even though he had many requests for papers at conferences or conventions. Soon I began receiving anxious letters that once again gave me an excuse to visit him in Swarthmore. I told him that they really did not expect him at his age to travel all the way to Pittsburgh for the meeting and that a short statement would be sufficient. We had a long talk about whether he should attempt something original or let his reputation rest on what he had published during the course of his career. I assured him that his reputation had been secured years before and that any new writing would be appreciated coming as it would from him, but that an extended or original piece was not necessary. For this occasion a brief statement of appreciation would be sufficient. He seemed relieved, but said he was still having problems organizing his thoughts. He showed me the several starts he had made. I offered some suggestions as I had for several other short pieces he had written in these last years, but the final version was completely his own.

His letter to the participants in the symposium read, in part:

> Even back in the [nineteen] twenties I was troubled lest the development of scientific studies in rhetoric should ignore values, and that we should become wholly an age of technology, a

collection of private interest groups that would have little interest in community values. I still cherish my hope that the revival of interest in classical rhetoric will maintain our interest in values, but I think we need to remember that the conflict between private interests and public values was present in Athens in the fifth century B.C.

The German romantic philosopher Friedrich Schlegel observed that every man is born a Platonist or an Aristotelian. But is it all temperament? Aristotle seems to contribute more and more to the development of contemporary rhetoric, and Plato less and less. I must confess to being born a Platonist and to being as often disappointed as he was at finding so little love of values in a world of facts. But we can now find among scientists and philosophers an increasing sense of the need for values if we are to prevent our modern civilization from bringing about its own destruction.

If we cannot turn readily to Plato's other world for the source of our values, we can find it in the developing interest in universal ideas, an inner light that will focus on values. We perhaps can learn to combine Aristotle's analytical intelligence with Plato's lofty view of the art of persuasion as it was seen in the mind of a generous philosopher. We shall not get so lost in the details of scholarship that we shall lose our larger vision of our duty in making this a better world.[21]

All the papers that had been submitted were sent to him. He was justly proud that a conference had been held in his honor. But privately he was not impressed with the papers: "I am continuing to read the Symposium papers, and I am in a quandary. I have read all the papers included in the program, and they are all scholarly, well written, but purely historical in point of view. They would get the support of classicists as well worthy of publication. I have now read many of the others. [S]ome of them are devoid of ideas, and few have interesting things to say about what influence Greek rhetoric ought to have today. They would not be so strongly endorsed by classicists as worthy of publication."[22]

What he did find delight in was writing each person who submitted a paper and asking how they first got interested in classical rhetoric, what their academic careers had been, and what use they make of classical rhetoric in their teaching? "I'm getting some interesting replies, some even seem romantic," he wrote. "One says he had a seminar with me in Hawaii in 1969, and another says his boss is the son of the first girl I ever went with, in the mountains of Kentucky. I am telling him I am delighted, but how in hell did he find that out?"[23]

Ever since I had delivered the paper on Hoyt Hudson at the 1978 meeting, Everett had been inquiring about when I would submit it for publication. Several years before he had arranged for Michael Hudson, Hoyt's son, to send me a large box of Hudson's manuscripts. Everett supposed that I would start writing right away about Hudson. Once I presented the paper on Hudson at the convention hardly a letter came without some mention of the essay. He was insistent that it be published. To prod me along he sent me every scrap of information he had about Hudson as well as pictures. Meanwhile I was working on it, when time from my academic and other duties permitted. Part of what held me up was that I was not as familiar with Hudson's background as I had been with Everett's. Ray Howes came to my rescue. He read various drafts and made helpful suggestions and corrections of fact that rounded out the essay to be more than a standard research article. Finally in 1982, it was published, and Everett wrote immediately: "The May *QJS* arrived yesterday morning, and I have spent all my time with it. My memories of Hoyt are so nostalgic that I cannot claim to be passing an intellectual judgment on the essay. And my love for his ideal and achievements as a man of letters are so deeply felt that I cannot say what the general reception of your essay may be. I can only say how much I admire the quality of your writing and the depth of your research into his works."[24] He asked for reprints which I ordered for him from the publisher and which he sent out to all sorts of institutions and people, including a surviving relative of Hudson's in New York. His love and admiration for Hudson was so great that I believe he appreciated this essay more than he did the one written about him. To show his appreciation he surprised me by sending me presentation copies of three of Hudson's books, each autographed and presented to Hunt: *The Praise of Folly*, Hudson's edition of John

Hoskins' *Directions for Speech and Style*, and a 1921 anthology *The Poet's Pack* that contained three of Hudson's poems including "Edward Arlington Robinson," the poem from which Hunt had quoted in concluding his eulogy of his dear friend in 1945. They remain prized possessions.

The final honor given to Hunt turned out to be the occasion for his final public statement on rhetoric. The year 1984 marked a very special anniversary for the Eastern Communication Association—its 75th. The convention returned to Philadelphia where the Association had been originally formed. It was a distinctive occasion, celebrating the Association's history and future. To commemorate this Diamond Anniversary, officers of the Association invited Everett Lee Hunt to attend and address the General Business Meeting on Saturday, March 10, as the oldest living member and Past President of the Association. Although he tired easily, he wrote and read a brief speech in which he turned to themes of a lifetime:

> I wish to express my gratitude for being invited to address the 75th annual convention of the Eastern Communication Association as its oldest living officer. I was President in 1923 and again in 1924, and I was editor of the *Quarterly Journal of Speech* from 1927-1930.
>
> Now may I say that it seems fitting to me that you should come back to Philadelphia to celebrate our declaration of Academic Independence. When Charles Woolbert and James O'Neill founded the National Association of Teachers of speech in 1915, they felt that the best program for academic independence was to be concerned with the scientific devotion to facts, with no concern for a content of opinions that might be controversial. When five years earlier, Paul Pearson founded the Eastern Association of Teachers of Speech he and his associates were concerned with platform and pulpit, and they studied the ideas and leaders of public opinion, such as William Jennings Bryan and other Chautauqua speakers.
>
> Ever since that time the association has been divided into a concern for scientific technology and a concern for ideas that form the public opinion of the world.
>
> The distinguished group of scholars who formed what became known as the Cornell school of rhetoric as a humane study were concerned with the subject matter of speeches that formed public opinion and they looked for what they called ideas that matter as a large part of the subject matter of their courses.
>
> With the development of scientific technology in this age of computerism the desire for the discovery and communication of accurate information replaces the search for persuasive ideas.
>
> One of the final subjects for the meeting of this convention is "Human Communication in the High Technological World of Tomorrow." This, I believe, is a danger signal, and I wish to urge that we regard the humane study of rhetoric as a great factor in the preservation of a liberal education.[25]

Such was his summary of his persistent thesis about rhetoric and education in his ninety-third year.

One year later, Thomas W. Benson of Penn State University recommended that the Eastern Communication Association create an award in Hunt's honor. The Executive Council agreed. The Everett Lee Hunt Scholarship Award was a tribute to his long service and distinguished career and was to be given annually to a member of the Association whose published research that year represented a commitment to excellence in scholarship. First presented in 1986, the Award memorialized Hunt's contribution to his profession. But, Hunt did not live to see the Award created or presented.

Near the end of April, 1984, Marjorie came home to find Everett stricken and lying prostrate on his bed. She called an ambulance and he was rushed to Taylor Hospital in nearby Ridley Park.

During the evening of April 30 as Marjorie was sitting with him, Everett became agitated because he could not speak distinctly. Marjorie suggested that they try to sing some vocal exercises she had taught him over the years. Once they began, Everett regained partial control of his voice and suggested a logical extension: "So long as we're singing, let's really sing." And with that, they really did sing, moving from one favorite old hymn to another, Marjorie and Everett singing together.

Shortly before midnight as he slept, Everett Lee Hunt slipped peacefully from this life.

Notes

[1] Hunt, "Rhetoric and Politics," *Pennsylvania Speech Annual: 25th Anniversary Edition, 21* (September 1964), pp. 10-16.

[2] *Ibid.*, p. 16.

[3] Typed "Final Paper for Speech 250" found in Hunt's copy of Public Speaking as a Liberal Art.

[4] Hunt summarized his view of the events at Cornell in a one page statement he entitled, "Speech at Cornell—A Brief Summary."

[5] Hunt, "The Humanities and the Performing Arts," manuscript of speech delivered at Cornell University, November 9, 1964.

[6] See the posthumously published version of that address, "General Specialists: Fifty Years Later," with brief introduction by Theodore Otto Windt, Jr., in *Rhetoric Society Quarterly, 17* (Spring 1987), pp. 167-176.

[7] Hunt, "Persuasion: Ancient and Modern," *Pacific Speech* (December 1966), p. 5.

[8] *Ibid.*, p. 7.

[9] Letter from Hunt to Windt, December 27, 1966.

[10] Hunt, "The Rhetoric of Violence," *California State Conference in Rhetorical Criticism*, papers of the conference (1969), p. 5. I am grateful to Professor Harold Barrett for sending me a copy of the speech, a tape recording of Everett's presentation, and for a variety of other materials dealing with this speaking tour.

[11] *Ibid.*

[12] Hunt, "Lincoln's Rhetoric Triumph at Cooper Union," in Lester Thonssen (ed.), *Representative American Speeches: 1969-1970, 42* (New York: H.W. Wilson, 1970), pp. 195-196.

[13] [Editor's preface], *ibid.*, p. 190.

[14] Letter from Towne to Hunt, January 6, 1971, quoted by permission of Dr. Ralph Towne.

[15] Hunt, "The Quaker Faith in Speaking Truth to Power," unpublished manuscript of speech given in Collection, October 1, 1964, pages not numbered.

[16] *Ibid.*

[17] Letter from Hunt to Windt, January 15, 1982.

[18] Letter from Governor Richard L. Thornburgh to Hunt, October 14, 1979.

[19] Letter from Hunt to Windt, October 16, 1979.

[20] "Ninety One Candles for Dr. Hunt," *The Swarthmorean* (October 24, 1980), clipping with no page number.

[21] Letter from Everett Lee Hunt to Professor Walter, Professor Enos, and the participants in the Symposium on Greek Rhetoric.

[22] Letter from Hunt to Windt, May 9, 1981.

[23] Letter from Hunt to Windt, second page of letter with first page and date missing, probably around the end of May 1981.

[24] Letter from Hunt to Windt, June 18, 1982.

[25] "Greetings to the 75th Annual ECA Convention," Philadelphia, March 10, 1983. There are four different versions of his short speech. His typing had seriously deteriorated and he added hand-written words that he had omitted when typing so that none of the copies is a clear text. I have collated the four into what I believe is the best representation of his remarks that day.

6

Epilogue

Teacher, writer, administrator, critic, counsellor, rhetorician, educational philosopher, horseman, mountain-climber, singer; in all these activities a self-styled "amateur," Everett Lee Hunt belonged to no pattern, no academic stereotype. He fashioned his own matrix; it left impressions of an uncommon diversity upon those who knew him or read his works. He devoted more than fifty years to higher education, first as a teacher of speech, later as professor of English and Dean of Swarthmore College. Rhetoric was his academic field. He served it long and well. The words of his one-time colleague at Cornell, Herbert Wichelns, deserve repeating: "the originality and subtlety of his insights did not lend themselves to systematic formulation . . . but his example of the true scholarly mind, inquiring, noting, combining, has put the present generation of graduate students and their teachers heavily in his debt."[1]

Everett often said that his life had been a series of accidents rather than one of conscious choices. Certainly, his moves from Huron to Cornell and then to Swarthmore as well as his changes from teacher of rhetoric to professor of English to Dean demonstrated that. Much as his career may have been dictated by circumstances, his thinking and teaching were guided by what interested him and by what he believed education ought to be and ought to achieve.

He began his career by objecting to limiting teaching in public speaking to drills in the mechanics of delivery and organization, but he soon expanded that criticism to those who were attempting to make teaching and research scientific. What he meant by scientific was taken from Woolbert, a quest for the facts and for certainty. Everett did not believe that anyone could be certain about how to teach a student to give a speech or about the issues that interested him, the issues of public policy, morality, goals for life and living, and a host of other issues that he came to call "general ideas," or "persistent questions for public discussion." These are perennial questions about which citizens must deliberate, debate, and decide. But they admit of no final answers, nor are they the exclusive property of experts.

In the ancient Greek rhetoricians he found the intellectual base and perspective for his approach to these general ideas. The ancients, particularly Aristotle and Isocrates, had divided issues into those that could be determined with rational certainty by dialectic and those that fell into the realm of probability, debatable issues that depend on rhetorical skill and personal intelligence to decide. But Hunt was seldom interested in historical or philological studies of the ancients. He sought to find a humane function for rhetoric in the modern world. That was his real focus throughout his life, and his persistence in calling himself an "amateur" rather than a professional emphasized that purpose. He wanted to use the perspective of classical rhetoric to roam over those general ideas whenever he was moved to do so, rather than settle down on an academic homestead to till a single piece of scholarly land. In sum, he wanted the profession to be creative and to take upon itself its public responsibilities beyond scholarship. But Hunt met resistance within his own profession. He was attempting to swim against the tide. American education, in general, and the discipline of public speaking, in particular, were becoming specialized and professional, the very antithesis of what he thought both ought to be. The tide and the undertow were stronger than he imagined. But despite resistance and ridicule, he remained steadfast.

Attempting to adjust to the proliferation of specialties, Hunt began to imagine an even larger purpose for rhetorical studies: to use rhetoric as an intellectual and humane instrument binding together the diverse fields of knowledge in a way that would give them a moral purpose and public significance. He repeatedly chided scholars—be they in scientific or humanistic fields of study—for studying smaller and smaller subjects, for scorning the public to write only for other specialized scholars, and for writing in an arcane jargon instead of literate English. But again he underestimated the prestige accorded the specialized expert and the honor heaped upon mystifying scholarship. Much to his dismay, he came to realize that few shared the high esteem in which he held the literate uses of language. In fact, reliance on technical writing and specialized jargon were logical results of the divisions of academic labor that professionalism had brought to colleges and universities in the twentieth century.

He was dismayed, but he did not despair. The rhetoric in which he believed and which he had fashioned was never a profession but a way of life, fully integrated into his teaching, his writing, and the ways in which he sought to live his life. The foundation of this rhetoric were the probabilities of life and issues. Quoting his beloved Koheleth and Ecclesiastes, he would say: "To everything there is a season, and a time for every purpose under the heavens."

The purpose of a humane rhetoric, as he conceived of it, was to assist free people to make free choices. Three qualities were necessary: imagination or intuition, reason, and sympathy. The ability to imagine different choices required wide reading and creative thinking. Because he held this quality in such high regard, he was the critic of anyone who presumed to have found the single method or way to seek truth or to resolve the persistent questions of public policy or the enduring problems of living. In this respect, he was humanistic skeptic who found all dogmatists—be they scientific or ideological or humanistic—threats to individual imagination and human freedom.

Imagination, however, had to be disciplined by intellect. Rational processes were necessary to help make the best guess among the many alternatives that the imagination had discovered. But Hunt was also skeptical of people becoming completely rational, and remained a gadfly repeatedly reminding himself and others of the limits of intellect. In his later years when he worked with the complex problems of students, faculty and administrators, he became even more convinced that an additional quality was needed for the full and healthy life. And he called that quality sympathy.

Hunt meant two different things by sympathy. First, he meant presenting ideas to others in a way that would appeal to their emotions as well as they minds. He wanted to treat people as whole, and intellect was only intellect, only the rational part, only a part of being whole and human. Second, he meant to have sympathy for the diverse opinions and feelings of others. It would have been a contradiction in his own humanism to insist that others agree with him. One could attempt to persuade others, but when one failed, one had to have the character and capacity to respect and attend to their reasons for disagreeing. In his Phi Beta Kappa speech at Queens College in 1962, he summarized many of these fundamental beliefs. He called his address: "Scholarship Versus Rhetoric in the Career of an Intellectual," and it was once again to Arnold that he turned for his model:

Matthew Arnold defended his right to give public judgment on a book in theology, not on the basis that he was a theologian, but on the grounds that his wide reading of the best that had been said and thought in the world gave him a knowledge of the healthy and unhealthy emotions which justified him in declaring this particular book unhealthy in its consequences. I suppose that Arnold's faith in the best that has been said and thought in the world is as good a source of general wisdom as any one can cite, but it has not saved some of his judgments from

Hunt

being ridiculed today as hopelessly Victorian. But we can still gain much even now by discussing his judgment in the light of changing times and customs. Perhaps this is as much truth as we can expect from an intellectual. By the very fact that the intellectual, even if he thinks with the learned, still wants to talk with the vulgar, he commits himself to statements about human nature and destiny which as yet are only probably true. And when he does this, he is in the realm best described and bounded in the beginning by Aristotle in his *Rhetoric, Ethics,* and *Politics*. Some will try to tell us that the realm of the probable is constantly being diminished by the discoveries of scientific certainties. But there is still reason for believing with Herbert Spenser that the constantly enlarging boundaries of the known only increase our contacts with the unknown. So long as we need to persuade men about making wise choices in the human situation, we will be helped by studying those who have reflected most deeply on the processes by which men were being persuaded to believe—Plato, Socrates, Aristotle, Cicero, Quintilian, Longinus, St. Augustine, Bacon, Milton, Burke.[2]

In this age of cultural and ethnic diversity such statements about the best that has been said and thought in the past may seem quaint, if not oppressive. But coming from Everett Lee Hunt they command our respect even when we cannot agree upon such matters. And such disagreements only point to the greater need for his humane rhetoric to help discuss and dispute these matters in a civil and civilized manner. The questions he posed and the way he posed them comprise the major questions asked by other educators during this turbulent century. What is an educator's primary responsibility: teaching or research? Will specialization or a liberal education best prepare our students for active participation in professional and public life? Can we find a method for intellectual discussion that helps in the search for truth while protecting the diversity of opinion necessary to keep the search lively? In sum, for what purposes do teachers teach and scholars do scholarship, and what kinds of students should we graduate and what kind of people do we want to become?

These questions admit no hard or final answers. They have continually been debated. As intellectual fashions have changed, so too have the answers. The answer upon which Everett placed the greatest value was the development of a humane rhetoric that would combine the human qualities of imagination, thought, and sympathy to free people to make their own individual choices. It was a perspective that allowed him to discern what he thought to be the enduring issues people should address; it was a method for ministering to them when his assistance was requested.

But perhaps I claim too much. Everett Hunt created no new theory of rhetoric. He developed no new method for criticism. He founded no system of scholarship which eager young scholars could apply. Indeed, had anyone called himself or herself a "Huntian" in his presence, he would have been sorely embarrassed.

He was more interested in questions than answers, more interested in exploring assumptions and purposes than in announcing conclusions.

During his 93 years he produced one landmark work of scholarship, "Plato and Aristotle on Rhetoric and Rhetoricians." But it was neither Plato nor Aristotle that he took as his guide in rhetorical matters. Instead, it was Isocrates and his theory of culture. Just as Isocrates sought to bind together Greeks against their common enemies, Hunt sought to bind together the separate and discrete compartments of knowledge in ways that would enrich the whole person and be of service to other people. His two essays on Matthew Arnold demonstrated the depth and breadth of his reading about Arnold, but they were written as much to defend himself as to explain how Arnold's thought could be related to rhetoric. The remainder of his published works, with the exception of *The Revolt of the College Intellectual*, were polemics about one current issue or another. In social matters, he was conservative; in politics, progressive; in professional matters of rhetoric and speech, a rebel.

But above all, he was a religious man. He was a Quaker and he brought many of those beliefs to his professional life and his writings on rhetoric. He delighted in the individual and the particular, the idiosyncratic and the personal. He summarized his theology in these words: "With Quakers, as with many contemporary thinkers, the transcendent God sitting on his throne in Heaven with his son Jesus at his side, is dead; he has become the immanent God within us, present in every man's life, lighting the inner light."[3] It was this inner light that directed and sustained him through personal and professional adversity. But that delight with the individual was balanced by an equally firm belief in service to others. It was in fusing these two Quaker beliefs combined with his classical studies that Hunt came to his vision of a humane rhetoric, one that would serve people more than professions, and to his own purposes in life. In this sense, Charles Woolbert, his early antagonist and later friend, was prophetic when he described Hunt as "a sort of lay pastor, an intellectual and spiritual knight errant, an educational court physician." As Everett himself sometimes remarked, the description turned out to be an accurate prophesy of his career.

Everett and Marjorie

But it was not only his commitment to a liberalizing rhetoric that marked Hunt as a distinctive voice in modern education. It was Everett Lee Hunt, the man, whose humane character spoke more eloquently than any words he wrote. In his speech at Queens College he said that the ethical appeal of a person's character is the most persuasive of all appeals and concluded by quoting his beloved Milton. The quotation he chose might well apply to him and his life: "He who would not be frustrate in his hope to write well in laudable things ought himself to be a true poem."

Notes

[1] Herbert A. Wichlens, "A History of the Speech Association of the Eastern States," published by the Speech Association of the Eastern States, April 1959, p. 7.

[2] Hunt, "Scholarship vs Rhetoric in the Career of an Intellectual," Phi Beta Kappa [address], Queens College of the City University of New York, May 11, 1962.

[3] Hunt, "Quakers and the *Bible*," unpublished speech read at discussion dinner, Whittier House, April 3, 1977.

Bibliography

A complete bibliography of Everett Lee Hunt's writings on rhetoric and public address can be found in my "Bibliography of Works by Everett Lee Hunt," *Rhetoric Society Quarterly, 14,* (Summer/Fall 1984), pp. 163-174. His writings on religion and other subjects are housed in the Friends Historical Library at Swarthmore College. All articles from the *Quarterly Journal of Public Speaking,* the *Quarterly Journal of Speech Education* and the *Quarterly Journal of Speech,* three different names for the same journal, are abbreviated to *QJS.*

I. Books

An Adventure in Education: Swarthmore College under Frank Aydelotte by The Swarthmore College Faculty. New York: Macmillan, 1942.

Auden, W.H. and Norman Holmes Pearson eds. *Poets of the English Language.* 4 vols. New York: Viking, 1950.

Baltzell, E. Digby. *Puritan Boston and Quaker Philadelphia.* Boston: Beacon Press, 1979.

Becker, Carl L. *Cornell University: Founders and the Founding.* Ithaca, NY: Cornell University Press, 1944).

Bishop, Morris. *A History of Cornell.* Ithaca, NY: Cornell University Press, 1971.

Blanchard, Frances. *Frank Aydelotte of Swarthmore.* Middletown, CT.: Wesleyan University Press, 1970.

Bledstone, Burton J. *The Culture of Professionalism: The Middle Class and the Development of Higher Education.* New York: W.W. Norton, 1976.

Bowen, Catherine Drinker. *Family Portrait.* Boston: Little Brown, 1970.

Brigance, William Norwood, Ed. *A History of American Public Address* (2 vols). New York: McGraw-Hill Book Company, Inc., 1943.

Brooks, Robert C. *Reading for Honors at Swarthmore.* New York: Oxford University Press, 1927.

Bryant, Donald C., *Rhetorical Dimensions in Criticism.* Baton Rouge, LA: Louisiana State University, 1973.

Bryant, Donald C. *The Rhetorical Idiom.* Ithaca, NY: Cornell University Press, 1959.

Cooper, Lane. *Experiments in Education.* Ithaca, NY: Cornell University Press, 1943.

Cooper, Lane. *Two Views of Education.* New Haven, CT: Yale University Press, 1922.

Cornell Alumni Association, *Our Cornell.* Ithaca, NY: Cornell Alumni Association, 1939.

Drummond, Alexander M. *A Course of Study in Speech Training and Public Speaking for Secondary Schools.* New York: Century Company, 1925.

Drummond, Alexander M. and Everett L. Hunt, eds. *Persistent Questions in Public Discussion.* New York: Century Company, 1924.

Eliot, T.S. *Selected Essays, 1917-1932.* New York: Harcourt, Brace, 1932.

Folsom, Franklin, ed. *The Window Reopened.* Koenig Alumni Center, Boulder, CO: UCB Alumni Association, 1978.

Gross, John. *The Rise and Fall of the Man of Letters: A Study of the Idiosyncratic and the Humane in Modern Literature.* New York: Macmillan, 1969.

Hochmuth [Nichols], Marie Kathryn, Ed. *A History and Criticism of American Public Address* (Vol. III). London: Longmans, Green, 1955.

Horton, Garner, Ed. *Pioneer College: A History of Pierre University and Huron College 1883-1958,* a special edition of the *Huron College Bulletin* (July 1, 1958).

Howes, Raymond F. *A Cornell Notebook*. Ithaca, NY: Cornell Alumni Association, 1971.

Howes, Raymond F., ed. *Historical Studies of Rhetoric and Rhetoricians*. Ithaca, NY: Cornell University Press, 1961.

Howes, Raymond F. *Important to Me*. Riverside, CA: privately printed, 1980.

Howes, Raymond F. *Notes on the Cornell School of Rhetoric*. Riverside, CA: privately printed, 1976.

Hunt, Everett Lee. *The Revolt of the College Intellectual*. Chicago: Aldine, 1963.

Lippmann, Walter. *A Preface to Politics*. New York: Mitchell Kennerly, 1913.

Lippmann, Walter. *Preface to Morals*. New York: Macmillan, 1913.

O'Neill, James Milton, ed. *Classified Models of Speech Composition*. New York: Century Company, 1922.

Perry, Bliss. *And Gladly Teach*. Reminiscences. Boston: Houghton Mifflin, 1935.

Perry, Bliss. *The Amateur Spirit*. Boston: Houghton Mifflin, 1904.

Reeves, Harrison Ross and Frank Humphrey Ristin. *Representative Essays in Modern Thought*. New York: American Book Company, 1913.

Studies in Rhetoric and Public Speaking in Honor of James Albert Winans. New York: Century Company, 1925.

Studies in Speech and Drama In Honor of Alexander M. Drummond. (Ithaca, NY: Cornell University Press, 1944.

Thonnsen, Lester and A. Craig Baird. *Speech Criticism*. New York: Ronald Press, 1948.

Wallace, Karl R., *History of Speech Education in America*. New York: Appleton-Century-Crofts, 1954.

Walton, Richard J. *Swarthmore College. An Informal History*. Swarthmore, PA: Swarthmore College, 1986.

Wichelns, Herbert A. *A History of the Speech Association of the Eastern States*. Mineola, NY: Speech Association of the Eastern States, 1959.

White, Helen C. *The Metaphysical Poets: A Study in Religious Experience*. New York: Macmillan, 1936.

II. Published Articles

"A Symposium on Rhetoric and General Education." *QJS*, *35* (October 1949), 419-426.

Arnold, Carroll C. "Rhetoric in America Since 1900" (pp. 3-7), in R.T. Oliver and M.G. Bauer (Eds.), *Re-Establishing the Speech Profession: The First Fifty Years*. No place of publication specified: Speech Association of the Eastern States, September 1959.

Davis, William H. "Courses for the Few or the Many," *QJS*, *9* (November, 1923), 358-362.

Drummond, Alexander M. "Graduate Work in Public Speaking," *QJS*, *9* (April 1923), 136-146.

Drummond, Alexander M. "Some Subjects for Graduate Study—Department of Public Speaking, Cornell University," *QJS*, *9* (April 1923), 147-153.

Heisey, D. Ray. "H.J.C. Grierson—Modern Scottish Rhetorician," *Western Journal of Speech Communication*, *30* (Fall 1966), 248-251.

Hicks, Granville. "Literature and Revolution," *English Journal*, *24* (March 1935) 219-239.

Hudson, Hoyt H. "The Field of Rhetoric," *QJS*, *9* (April 1923), 167-180.

Hunt, Everett Lee. "Academic Public Speaking," *QJS*, *3* (January 1917), 27-36.

Hunt, Everett Lee. "Adding Substance to Form in Public Speaking," *QJS*, *8* (June 1922), 256-265.

Hunt, Everett Lee. "An Adventure in Philosophy," *QJS*, *3* (October 1917), 297-303.

Hunt, Everett Lee. "Content and Form," *QJS*, *9* (November 1923), 324-329.

Hunt, Everett Lee. "Creative Teaching in Wartime," *QJS*, *4* (October 1918), 386-397.

Hunt, Everett Lee. "Dialectic: A Neglected Mode of Argument," *QJS*, *7* (June 1921), 221-232.

Hunt, Everett Lee. "Frank Aydelotte," *Swarthmore College Bulletin, Alumni Issue*, (February 1957), 5, 28-31.

Hunt, Everett Lee. "From Rhetoric Deliver Us," *QJS*, *14* (April 1928), 261-268.

Hunt, Everett Lee. "General Specialists," *QJS*, *2* (July 1916), 252-263.

Hunt, Everett Lee. "General Specialists: Fifty Years Later," *Rhetoric Society Quarterly* (Spring 1987), 167-176.

Hunt, Everett Lee. "Hoyt Hopewell Hudson," *QJS, 31* (October 1945), 272-274.

Hunt, Everett Lee. "Humanism and Dogma," *Sewanee Review, 43* (1935), 501-503.

Hunt, Everett Lee. "Knowledge and Skill," *QJS, 9* (February 1923), 67-76.

Hunt, Everett Lee. "Lincoln's Rhetorical Triumph at Cooper Union" (pp.189-196), in *Representative American Speeches: 1969-1970*, ed. by Lester Thonnsen. New York: H.W. Wilson, 1970.

Hunt, Everett Lee. "Matthew Arnold and His Critics," *Sewanee Review, 44* (October-December 1936), 449-467.

Hunt, Everett Lee. "Matthew Arnold: The Critic as Rhetorician," *QJS, 20* (November 1934), 483-507.

Hunt, Everett Lee. "Music in a Liberal Arts College" (pp. 22-26), in *Society for Music in a Liberal Arts College*, 7th annual meeting, Princeton University, proceedings, 1956.

Hunt, Everett Lee. "Nason at Swarthmore," *Swarthmore College Bulletin Alumni Issue*, (February 1953), 1-2.

Hunt, Everett Lee. "Persuasion: Ancient and Modern," *Pacific Speech*, (December 1966), 5-8.

Hunt, Everett Lee. "Reading for Honors and Common Sense," *School and Society*, 42 (November 30, 1935), 726-732.

Hunt, Everett Lee. "Rhetoric and General Education," *QJS, 35* (October 1949), 275-279.

Hunt, Everett Lee. "Rhetoric and Politics," *Pennsylvania Speech Annual, 21* (September 1964), 10-16.

Hunt, Everett Lee. "Rhetoric as a Humane Study," *QJS, 41* (April 1955), 114-117.

Hunt, Everett Lee. "The Dean and the Psychiatrist," *Mental Health, 37* (April 1953), 177-196.

Hunt, Everett Lee. "The Rhetoric of Violence" (pp. 1-5), in *California State [University-Hayward] Conference in Rhetorical Criticism*, ed. by James Johnson. (1969).

Hunt, Everett Lee. "The Rhetorical Mood of World War II," *QJS, 29* (February 1943), 1-5.

Hunt, Everett Lee. "The Scientific Spirit in Public Speaking," *QJS, 1* (July 1915), 185-193.

Hunt, Everett Lee. "The Social Interpretation of Literature," *English Journal, 24* (March 1935), 214-219.

Hunt, Everett Lee. "Thinking about Feeling," *Swarthmore College Bulletin Alumni Issue*, (May 1958), 2-4, 29.

Mabie, E.C. "Speech From Another Angle," *QJS, 9* (November 1923), 330-333.

O'Neill, James M. "Speech Content and Course Content," *QJS, 9* (February 1923), 25-52.

O'Neill, James M. Review of Public Speaking, *QJS, 2* (April 1916), 213-215.

Reid, Loren, "James Albert Winans (1872-1956)," *Southern Speech Communication Journal, 31* (1982), 89-117.

Research Committee [of the National Association of Academic Teachers of Public Speaking]. "Research in Public Speaking," *QJS, 1* (April-October 1915), 24-32.

"Rhetoric and General Education: A Symposium Continued." *QJS, 36* (February 1950), 1-19.

Sandford, W.P., "The Problems of Speech Content," *QJS, 8* (November 1922), 364-371.

Shorey, Paul. "What Teachers of Speech May Learn from the Theory and Practice of the Greek," *QJS, 8* (April 1922), 105-132.

Simrell, V.C. "Mere Rhetoric," *QJS, 9* (June 1928), 359-374.

Ullman, Eliza Ulrich. "Swarthmore Chautauqua," *Swarthmore College Bulletin* (January 1975), 20-23.

Wichelns, Herbert A. "Our Hidden Aims," *QJS, 9* (November 1923), 315-323.

Winans, James A. "Speech," *QJS, 9* (June 1923), 223-231.

Winans, James A. "The Need for Research," *QJS, 1* (April-October 1915), 17-23.

Windt, Jr., Theodore Otto. "Everett Lee Hunt on Rhetoric," *Speech Teacher* (September 1972), 177-192.

Windt, Jr., Theodore Otto. "Hoyt H. Hudson: Spokesman for the Cornell School of Rhetoric," *QJS, 67* (October 1982), 186-200.

Woolbert, Charles H. "A Problem in Pragmatism," *QJS, 2* (July 1916), 264-274.

Woolbert, Charles H. "The Organization of Departments of Speech Sciences in Universities," *QJS, 2* (January 1916), 64-77.

III. Unpublished Works

Black, Edwin, "Herbert A. Wichelns and Effects," paper delivered in honor of Herbert A. Wichelns at the annual meeting of the Speech Communication Association, 1989.

Bryant, Donald C., "The Founders of the Cornell Tradition of Rhetorical Study," paper presented at the annual meeting of the Speech Association of America, 1957.

Condon, Denis. *Foundations of the Cornell School of Rhetoric*, unpublished Ph.D. dissertation, University of Pittsburgh, 1988.

Howell, Wilbur Samuel, "Everett Hunt at Cornell: A Personal Recollection," November 4, 1989.

Hunt, "Greetings to the 75th Annual ECA Convention," 1983, 1 page, but several different versions.

Hunt, Everett Lee. "In the Days of My Youth," (notebook) n.d., n.p.

Hunt, Everett Lee. "Rhetoric and Literary Criticism," lecture at George Washington University, 1958, 18 pages.

Hunt, Everett Lee. "Scholarship vs. Rhetoric in the Career of an Intellectual," Phi Beta Kappa Address, Queens College, 1962, 11 pages.

Hunt, Everett Lee. "Speech at Cornell—A Brief Summary," 1966, 1 page

Hunt, Everett Lee. *Studies in Rhetoric*, n.d., n.p.

Hunt, Everett Lee. "The Cornell School of Humane Rhetoric," 1981, 3 pages.

Hunt, Everett Lee. "The Fiftieth Reunion of the Class of 1928," 1978, 1 page.

Hunt, Everett Lee. "The Humanities and the Performing Arts," speech delivered at Cornell University, 1964, 14 pages.

Hunt, Everett Lee. "The Quaker Faith in Speaking Truth to Power," October, 1964, n.p.

King, C. Harold, "This Man, Hunt," paper read by Carroll Arnold at panel honoring Everett Lee Hunt at the annual meeting of the Speech Communication Association, December 1959.

Rasmussen, Donald W., *A History of Speech Education at Huron College 1883-1943*, unpublished M.A. thesis, University of South Dakota, 1949.

IV. Taped Recordings

Audio recording of Everett Lee Hunt, August 10, 1967.

Audio recording of Everett Lee Hunt's "The Rhetoric of Violence," California State University at Hayward, 1969.

Audio recording of Everett Lee Hunt's seminar on humanism in rhetoric at Temple University, July, 1971.

About the Author

Theodore Otto Windt, Jr.

Dr. Theodore Otto Windt, Jr. is Associate Professor of Political Rhetoric in the Department of Communication at the University of Pittsburgh. He is one of the Chancellor's Distinguished Teachers of the University. He also serves on the Governing Board of the Institute of Politics. He is political commentator on national politics for "Weekend Magazine" on KDKA-TV and for KQV radio.

Dr. Windt, a native Texan, received his B.A. degree in English and Speech from Texas Lutheran College; his M.A. in Theatre Arts from Bowling Green State University; and his Ph.D. in Rhetoric and Theatre with collateral work in Philosophy from Ohio State University. He taught at Temple University and the University of Texas (El Paso) before coming to the University of Pittsburgh.

Dr. Windt is the editor of *Presidential Rhetoric: 1961 to the Present*; co-editor with his wife, Beth Ingold, of *Essays in Presidential Rhetoric*; and the author of *Presidents and Protesters: Political Rhetoric in the 1960s*.

In addition to his writing and academic duties, Dr. Windt is a professional speech writer and political consultant. He served as Richard L. Thornburgh's chief speech writer in the successful 1978 campaign for Governor of Pennsylvania. He has been an associate of Matt Reese Communications and worked with Kitchens and Associates as well as Southern Strategies, all political and public affairs consulting firms. Dr. Windt specializes in overall communication strategy in campaigns and in television debates. He also works in the corporate community as a communications consultant. Among his clients have been Rockwell International and ALCOA.

During 1987 and 1988, he joined fifteen other nationally prominent journalists and academics to serve on the Harvard Commission on Presidential Press Conferences, chaired by Marvin Kalb of the Joan Shorenstein Barone Center for the Study of Press, Politics and Public Policy at the John F. Kennedy School of Government. Recommendations from the Report on the Commission were implemented by President George Bush.

Dr. Windt was a close friend of Everett Hunt during the last twenty years of Hunt's life. Mrs. Marjorie Hunt designated him as Dean Hunt's biographer.

Dr. Windt resides with his wife, Beth Ingold, in the Fox Chapel area of Pittsburgh. He has two sons, Ted III, and Thad.